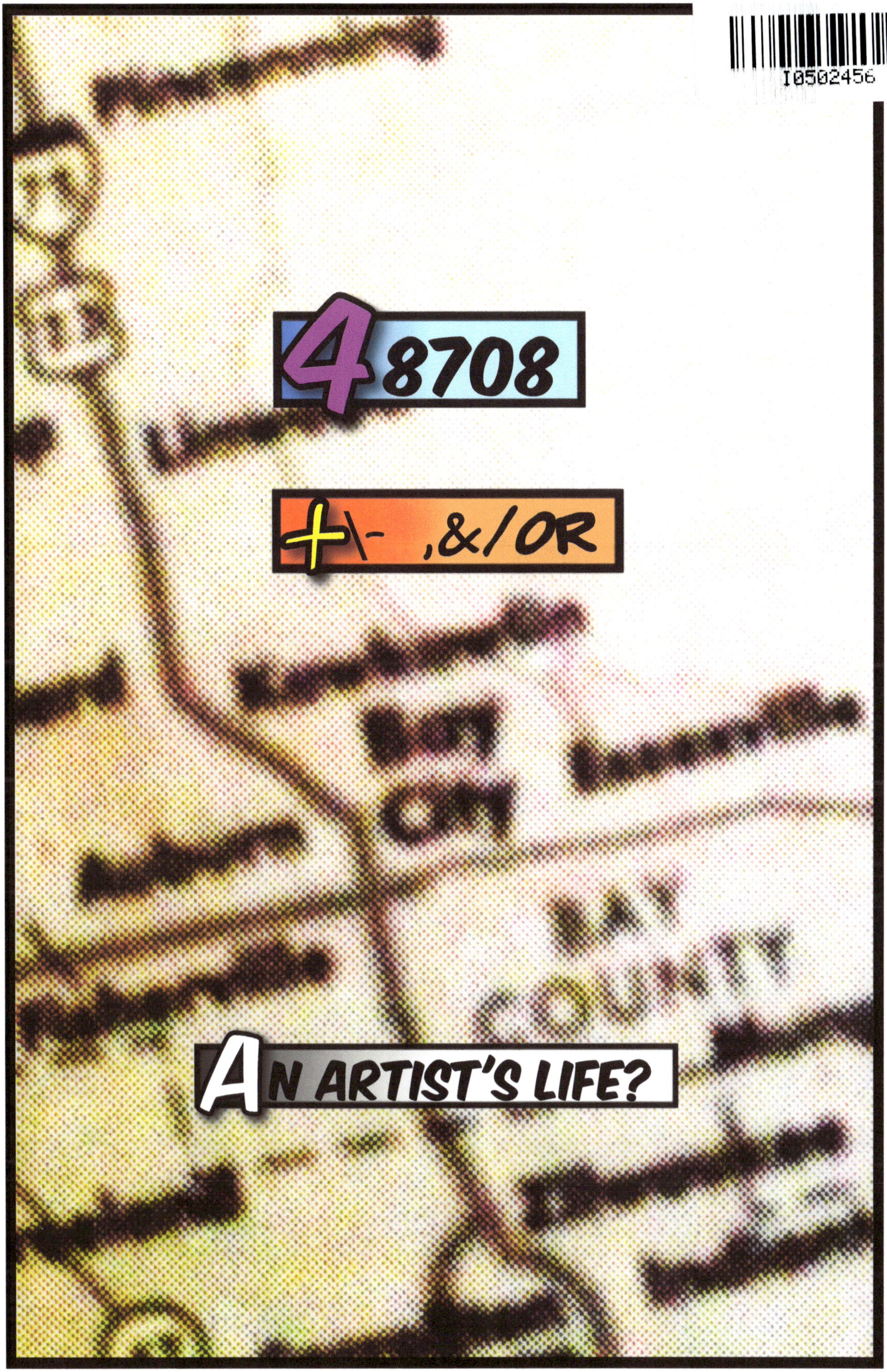

48708

+\- ,&/OR

AN ARTIST'S LIFE?

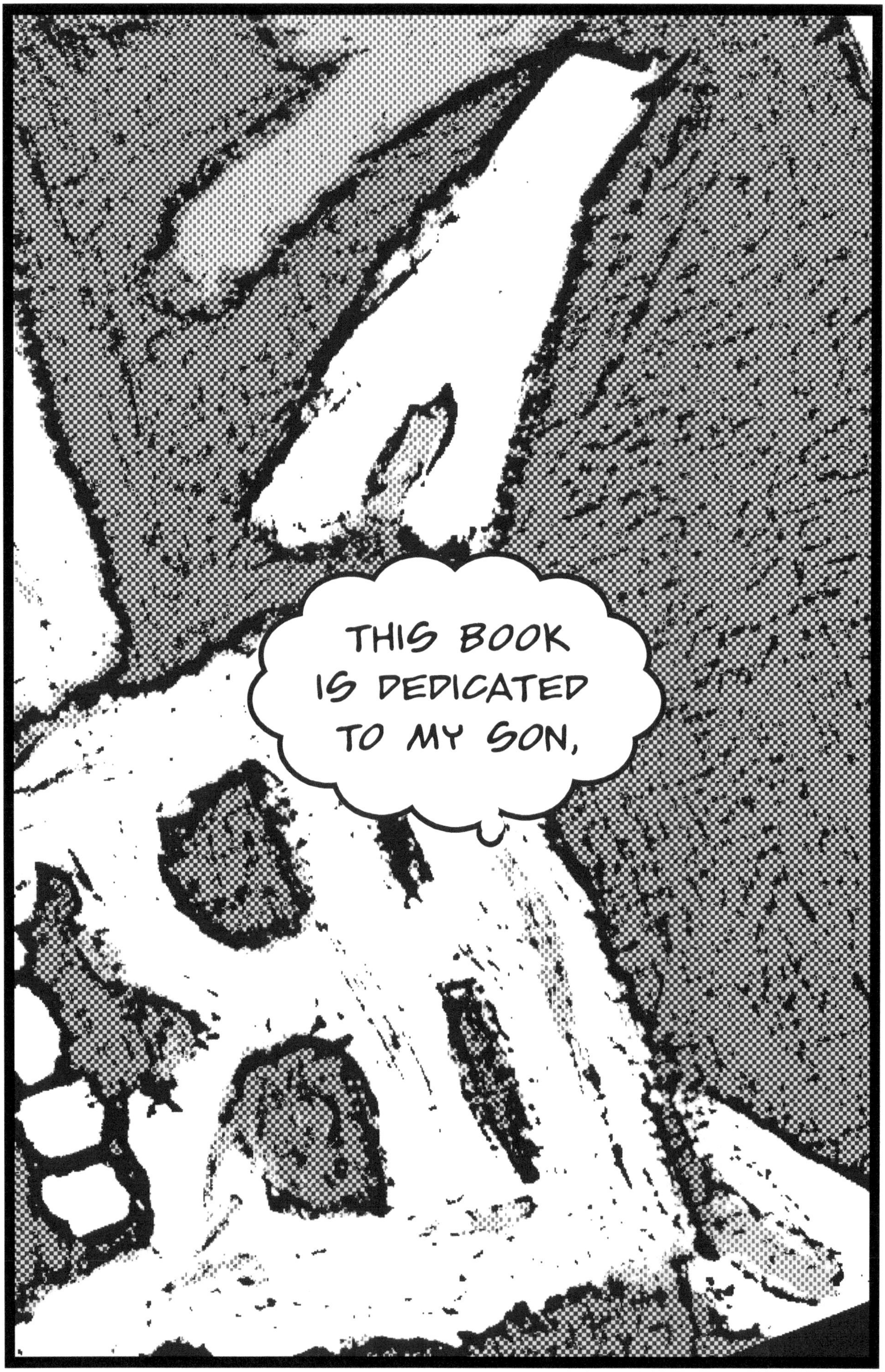
THIS BOOK IS DEDICATED TO MY SON,

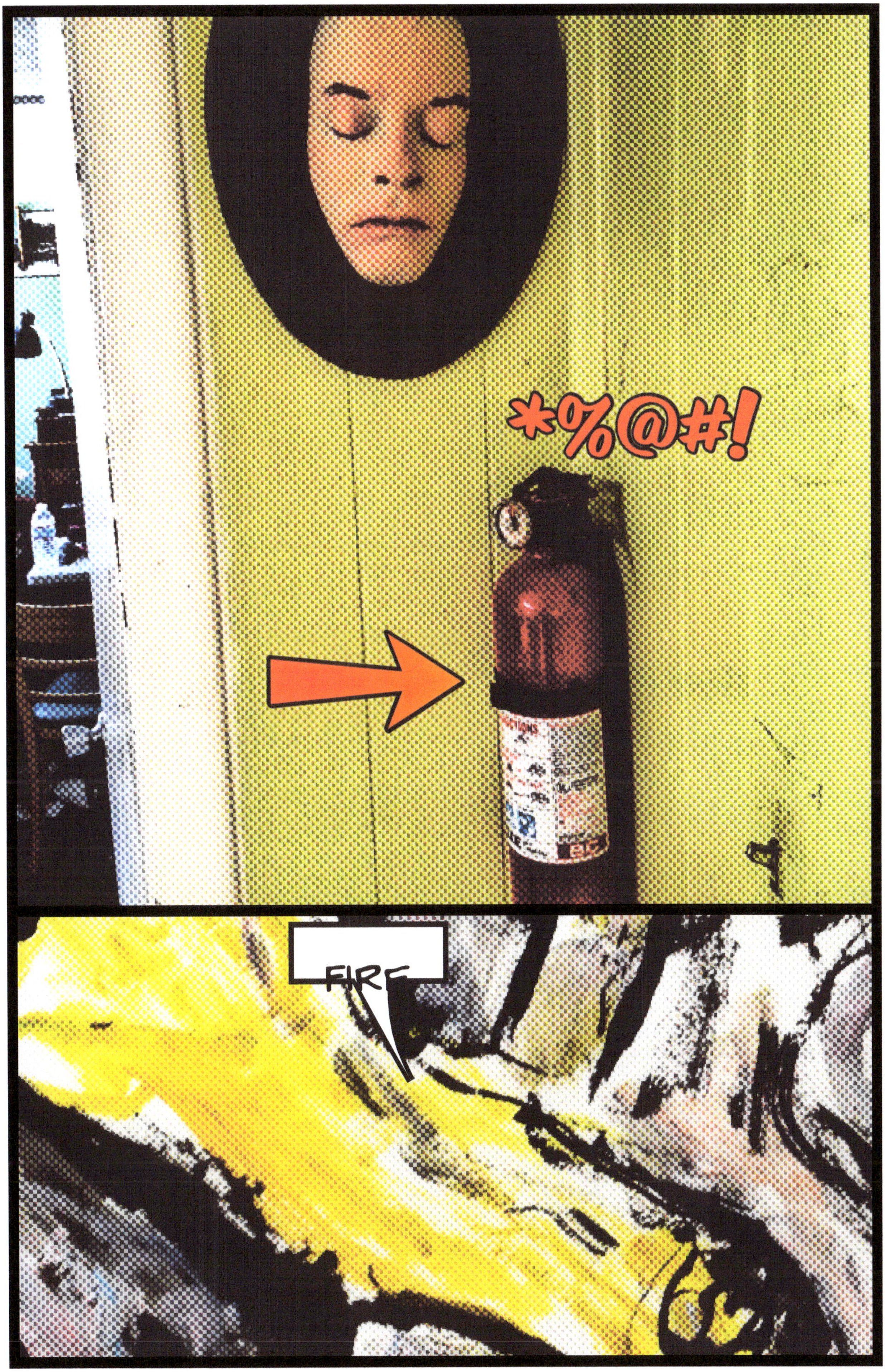
*%@#!
FIRE

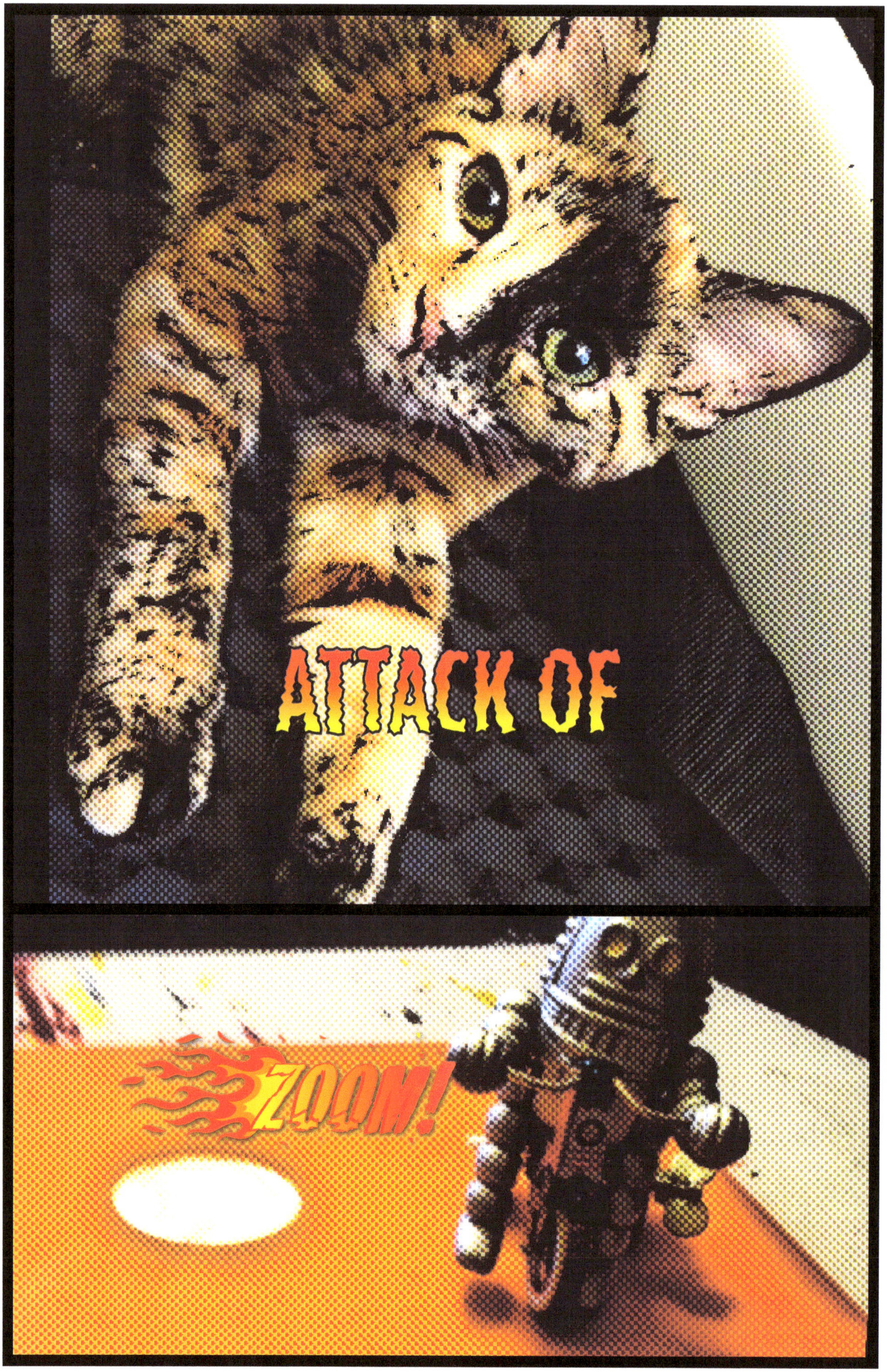
ATTACK OF
ZOOM!

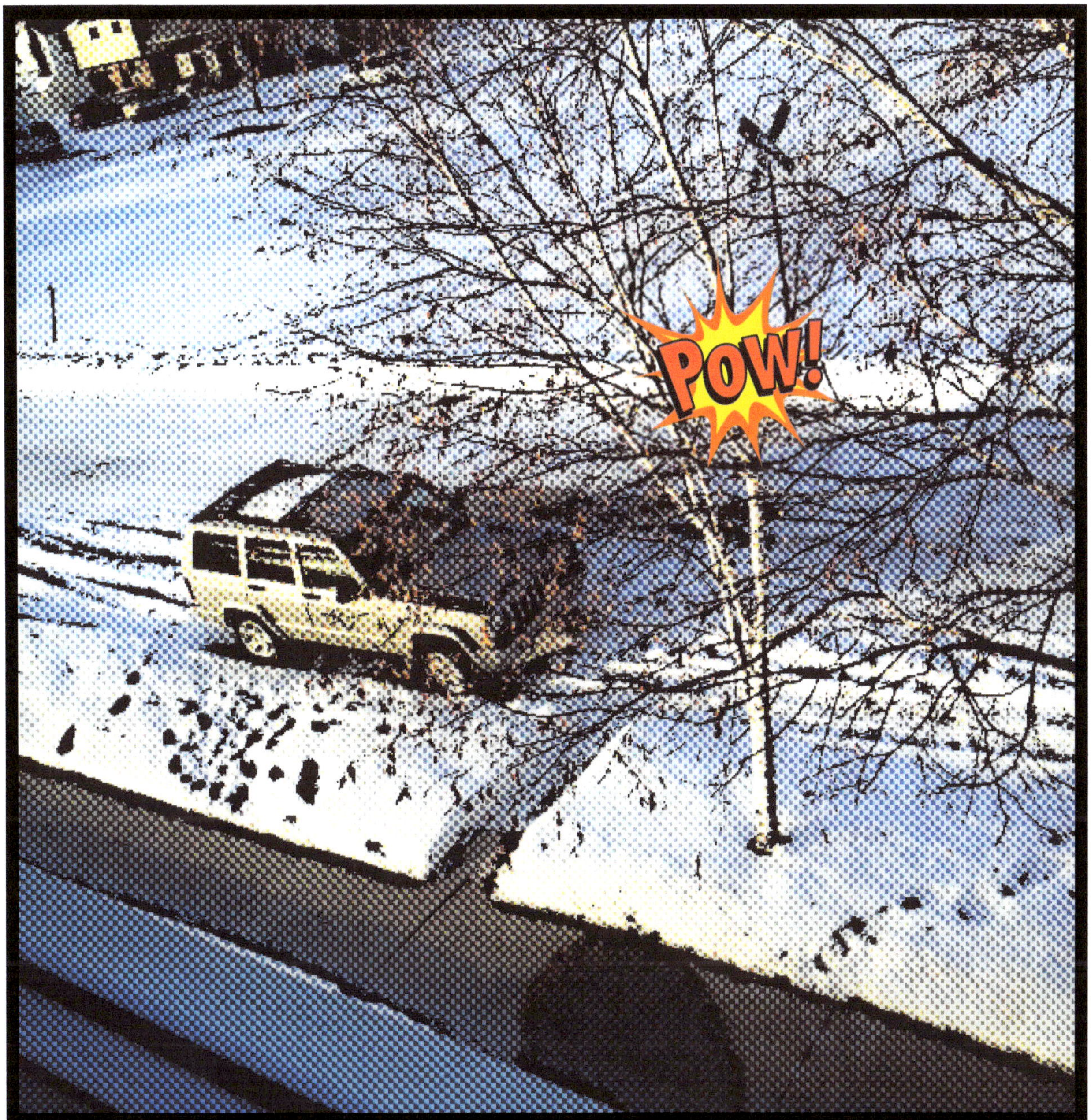
POW!
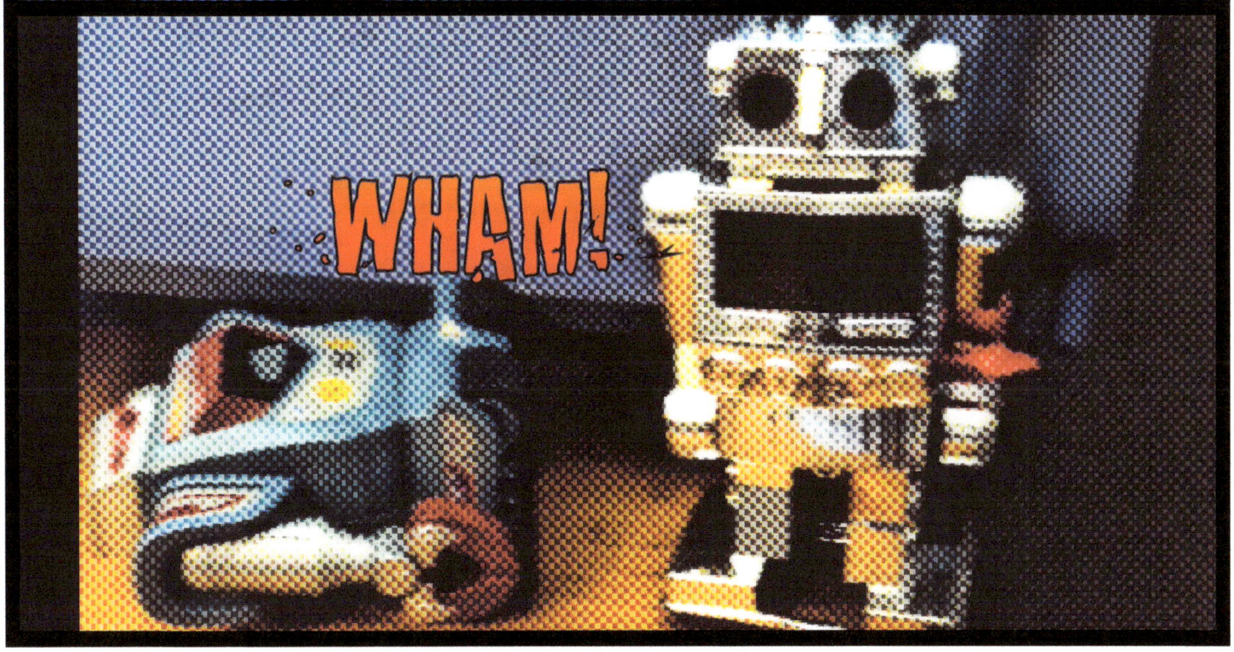
WHAM!

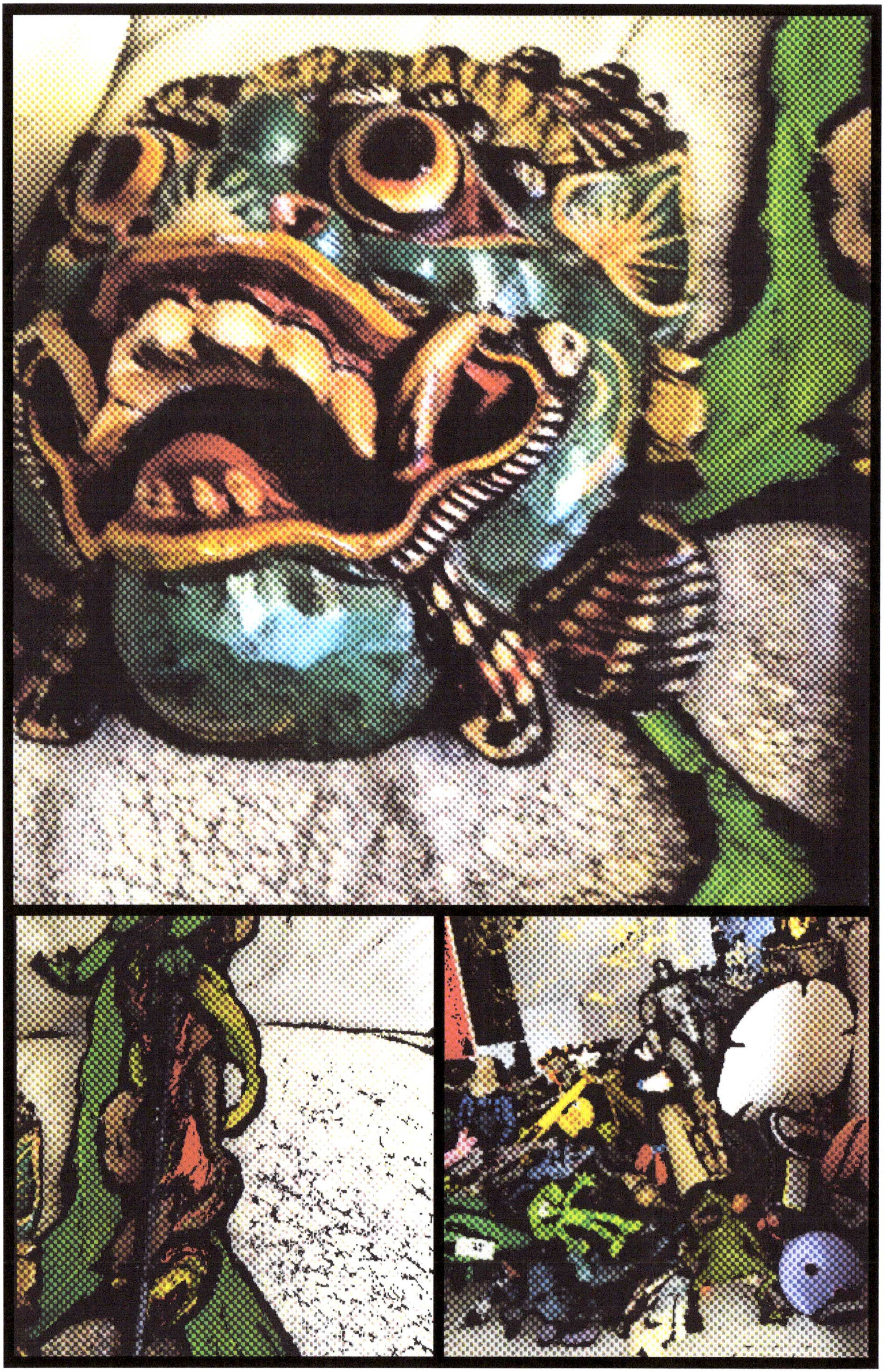

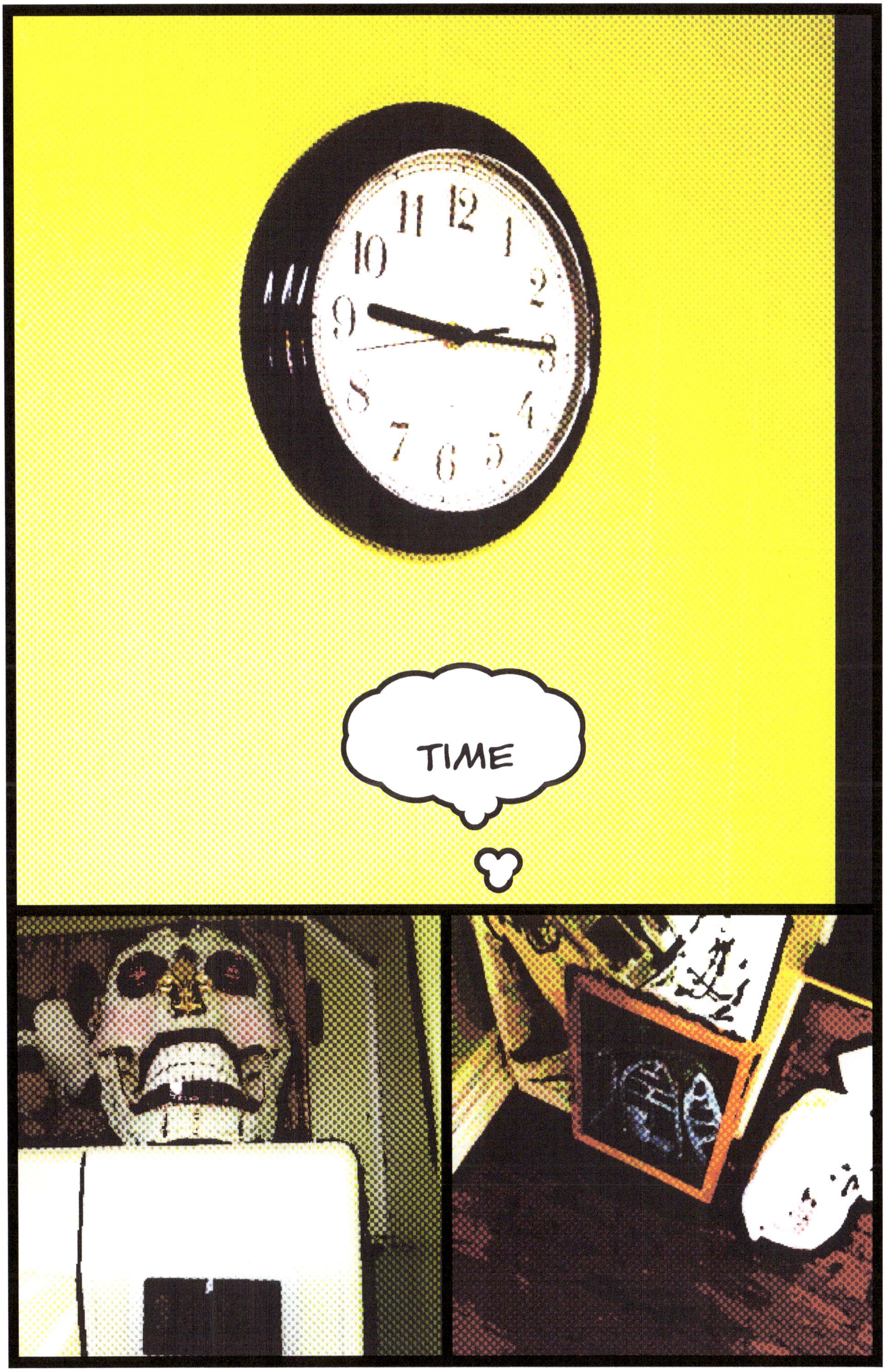
TIME

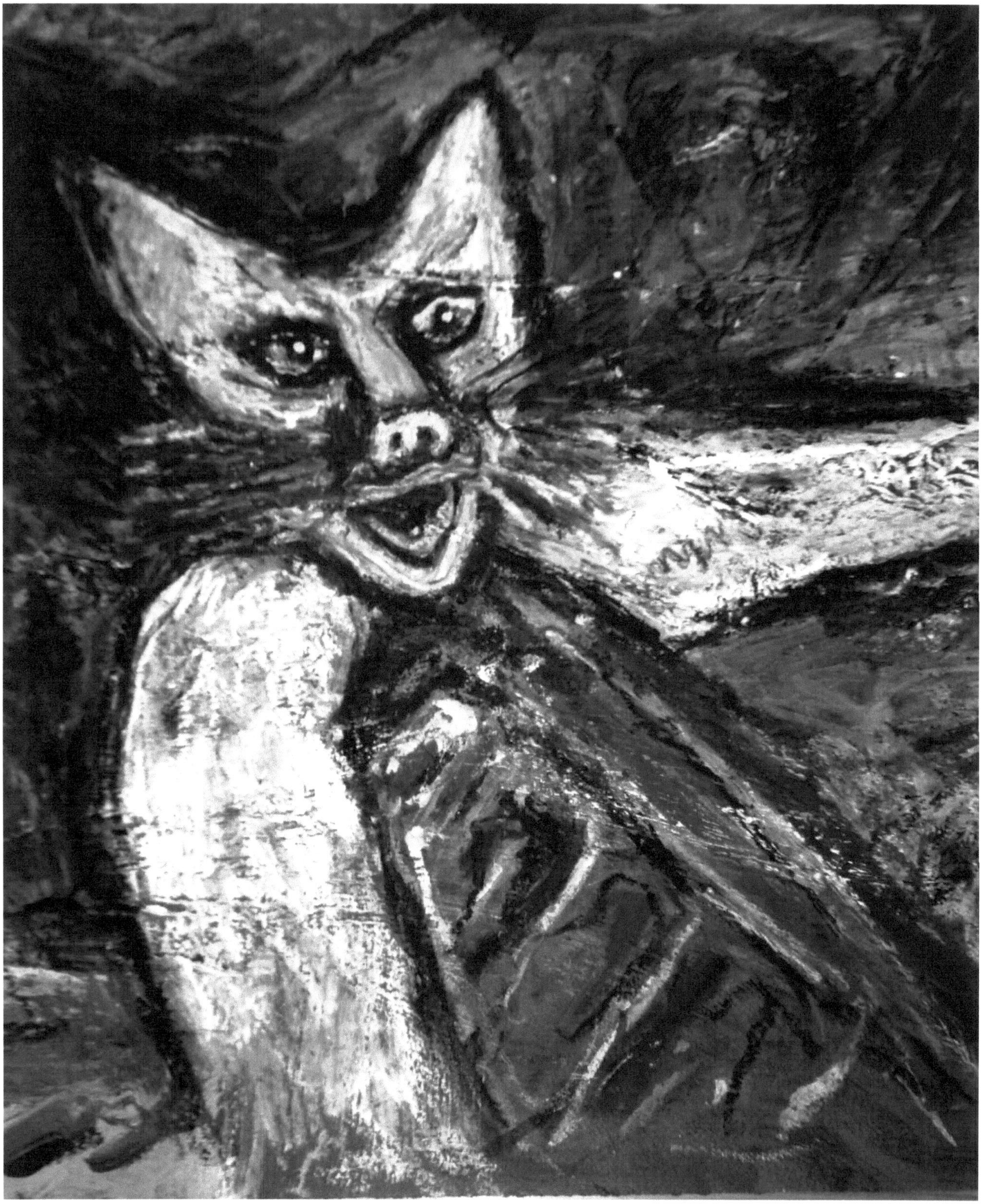

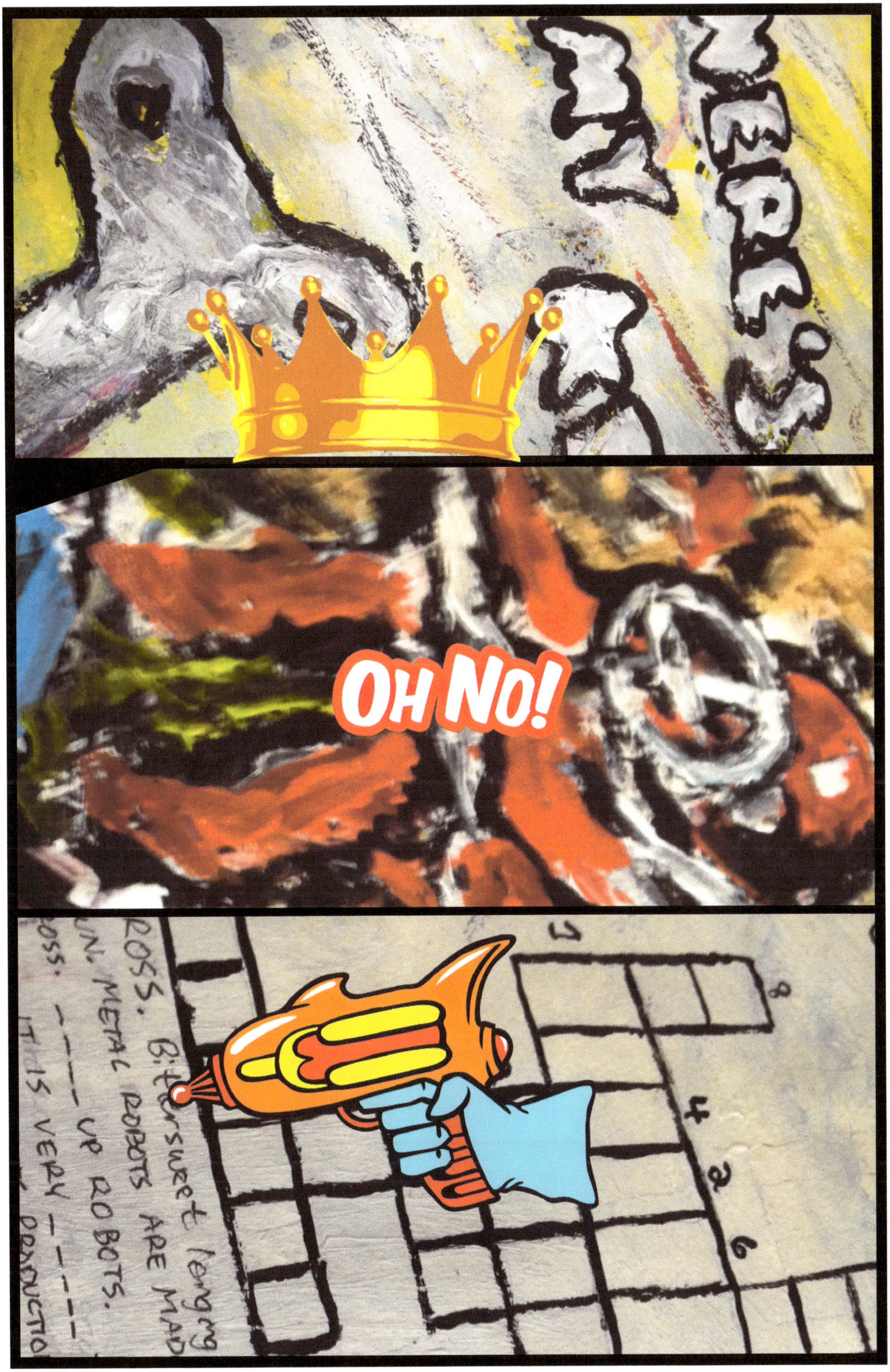
OH NO!

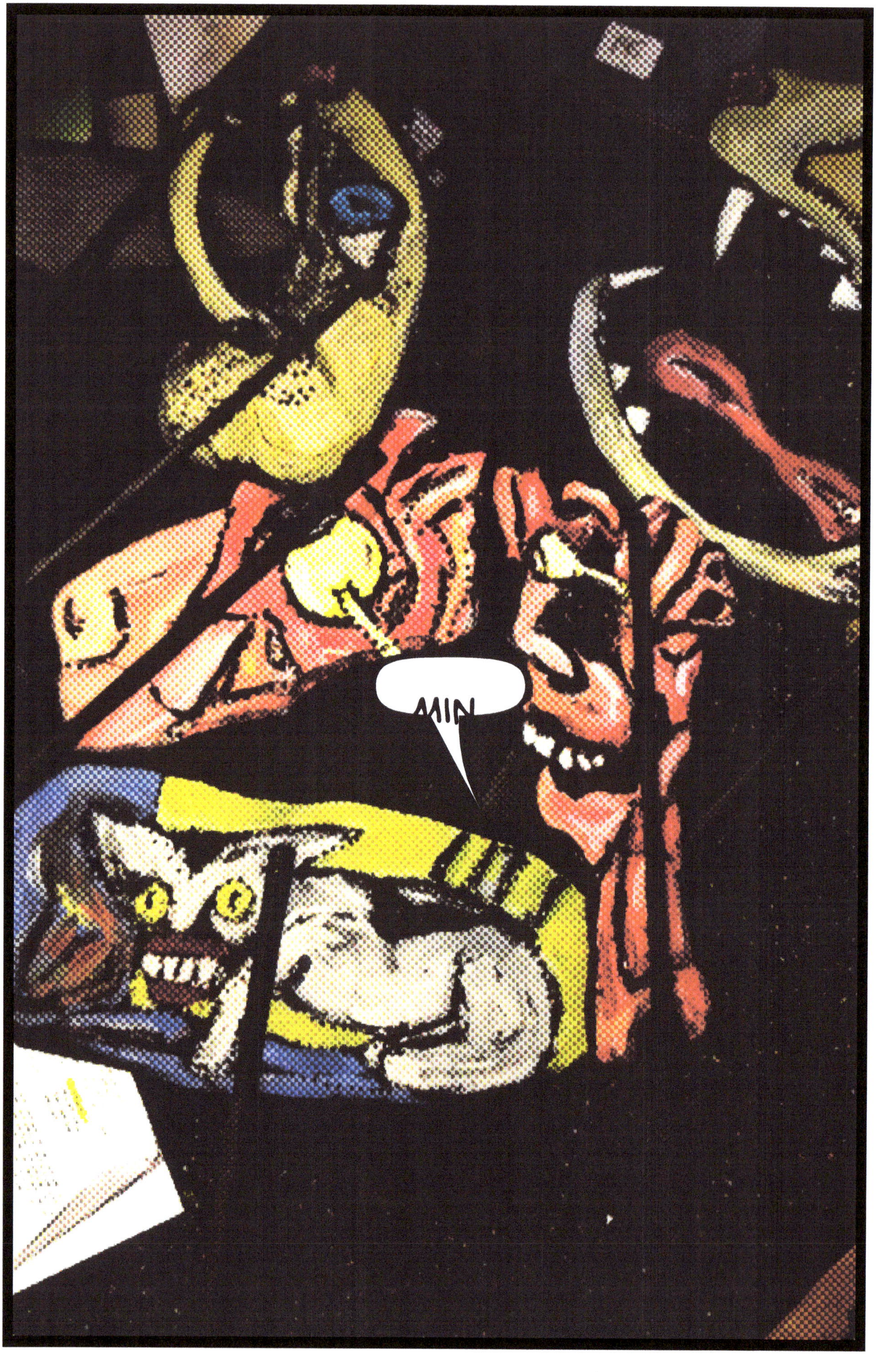
MIN

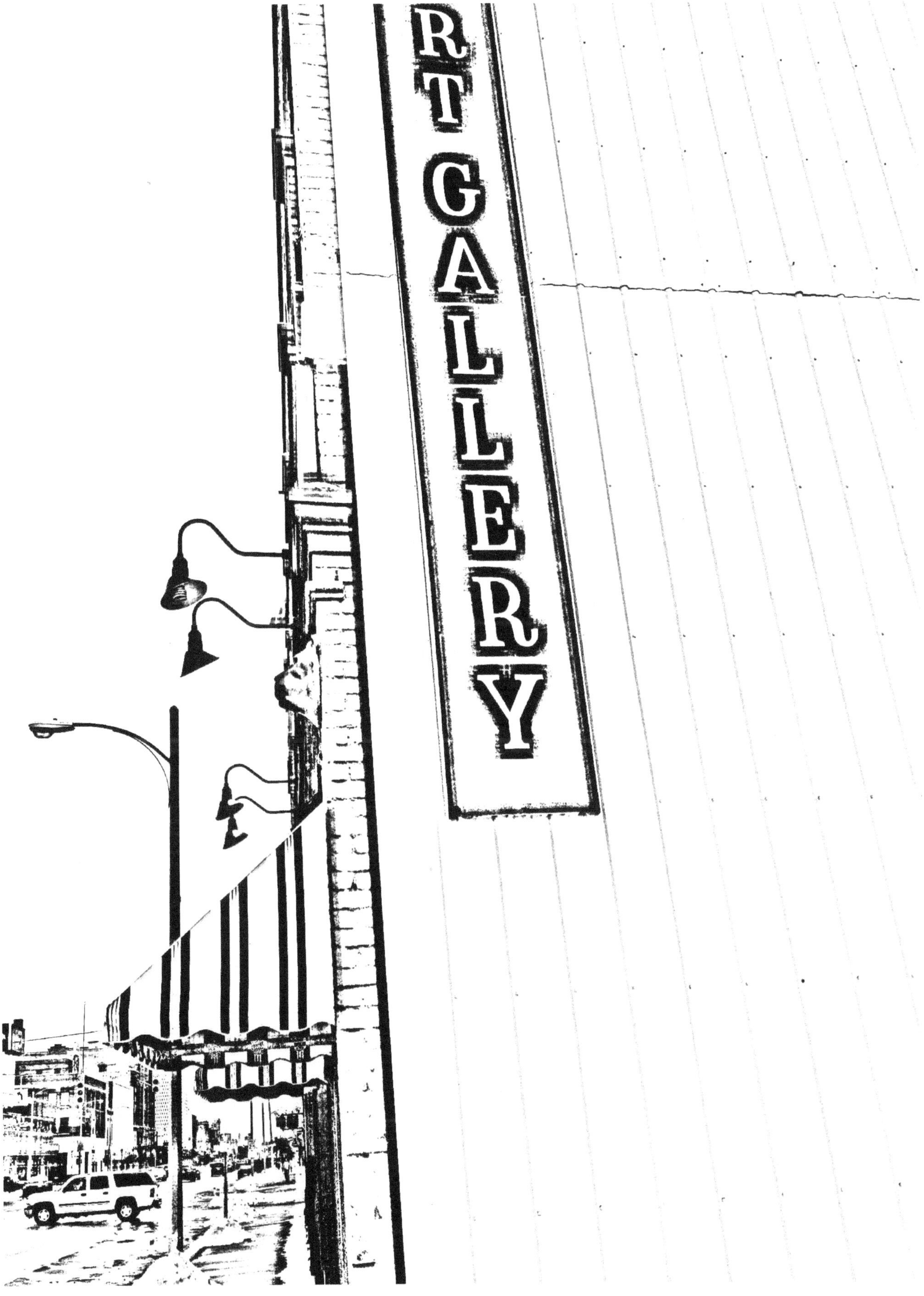
RT GALLERY

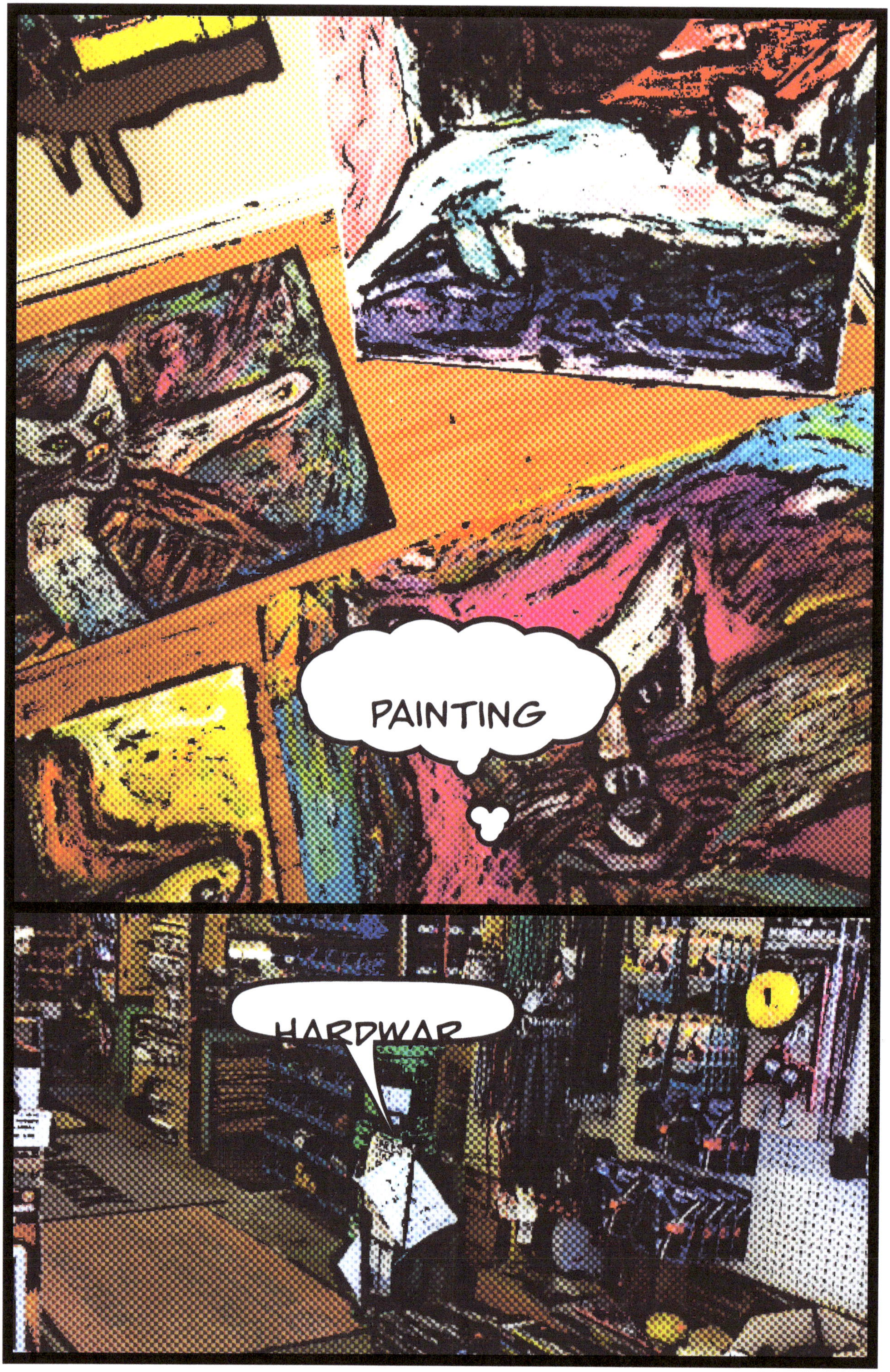
PAINTING
HARDWAR

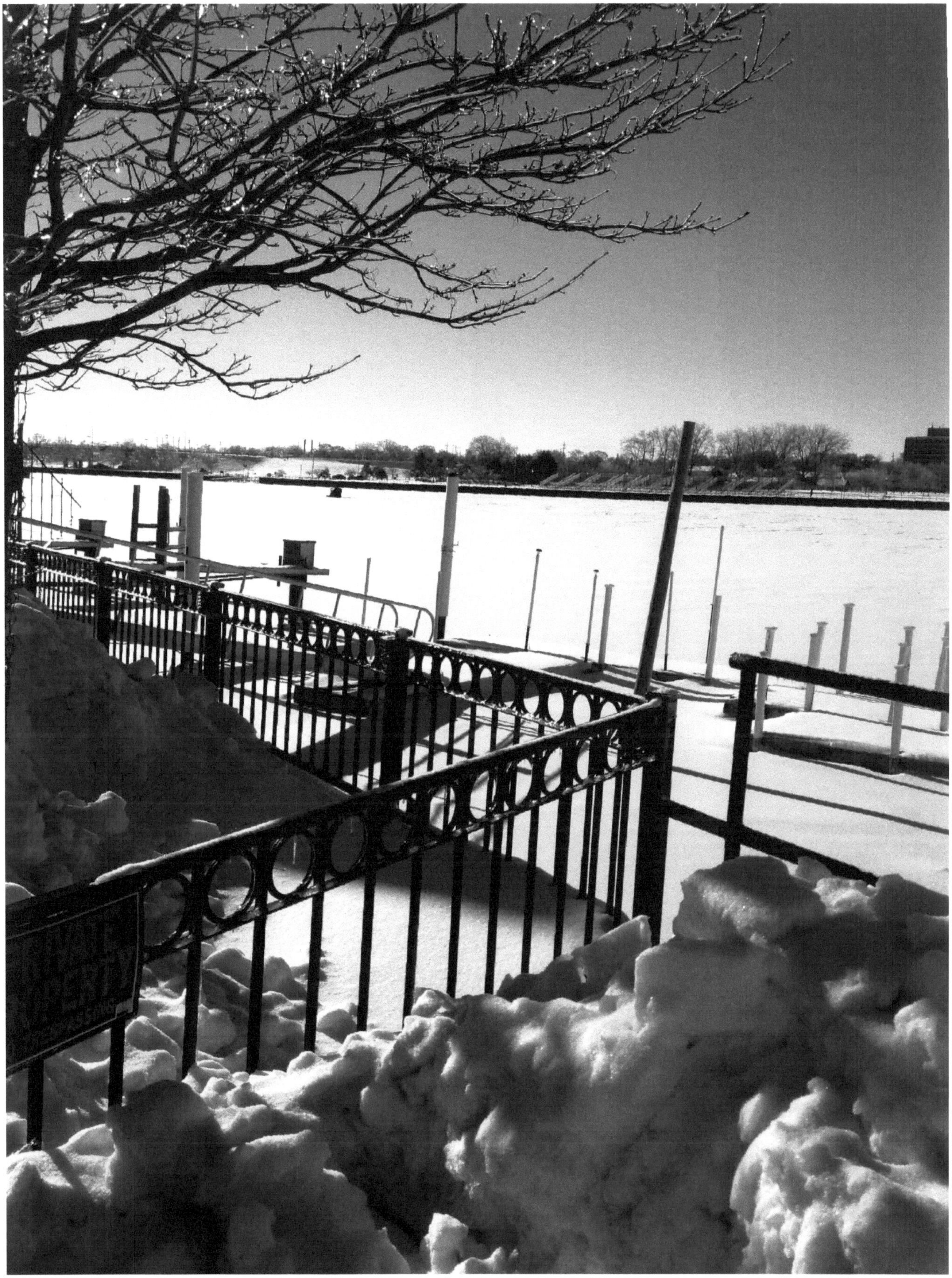

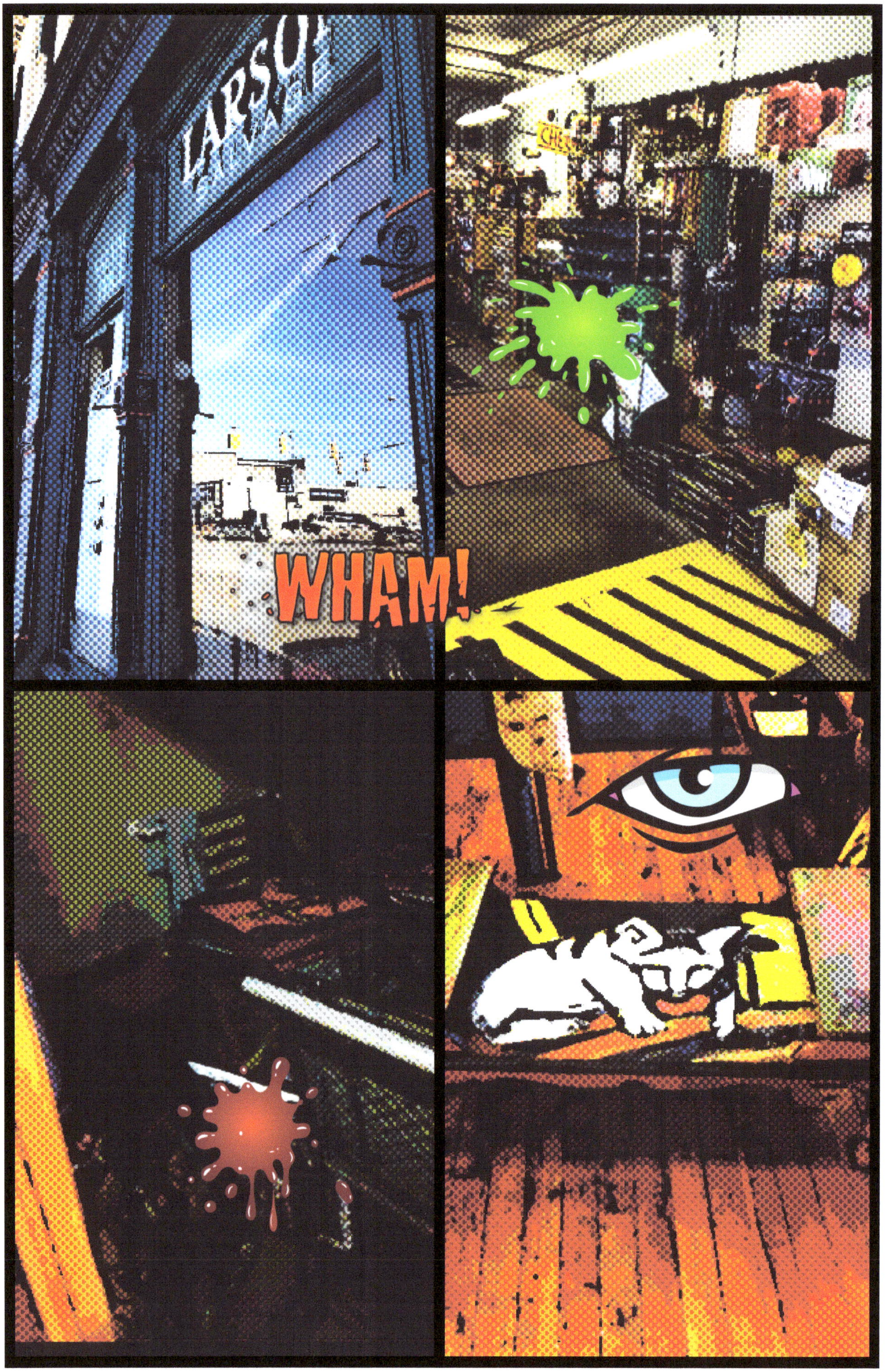
WHAM!

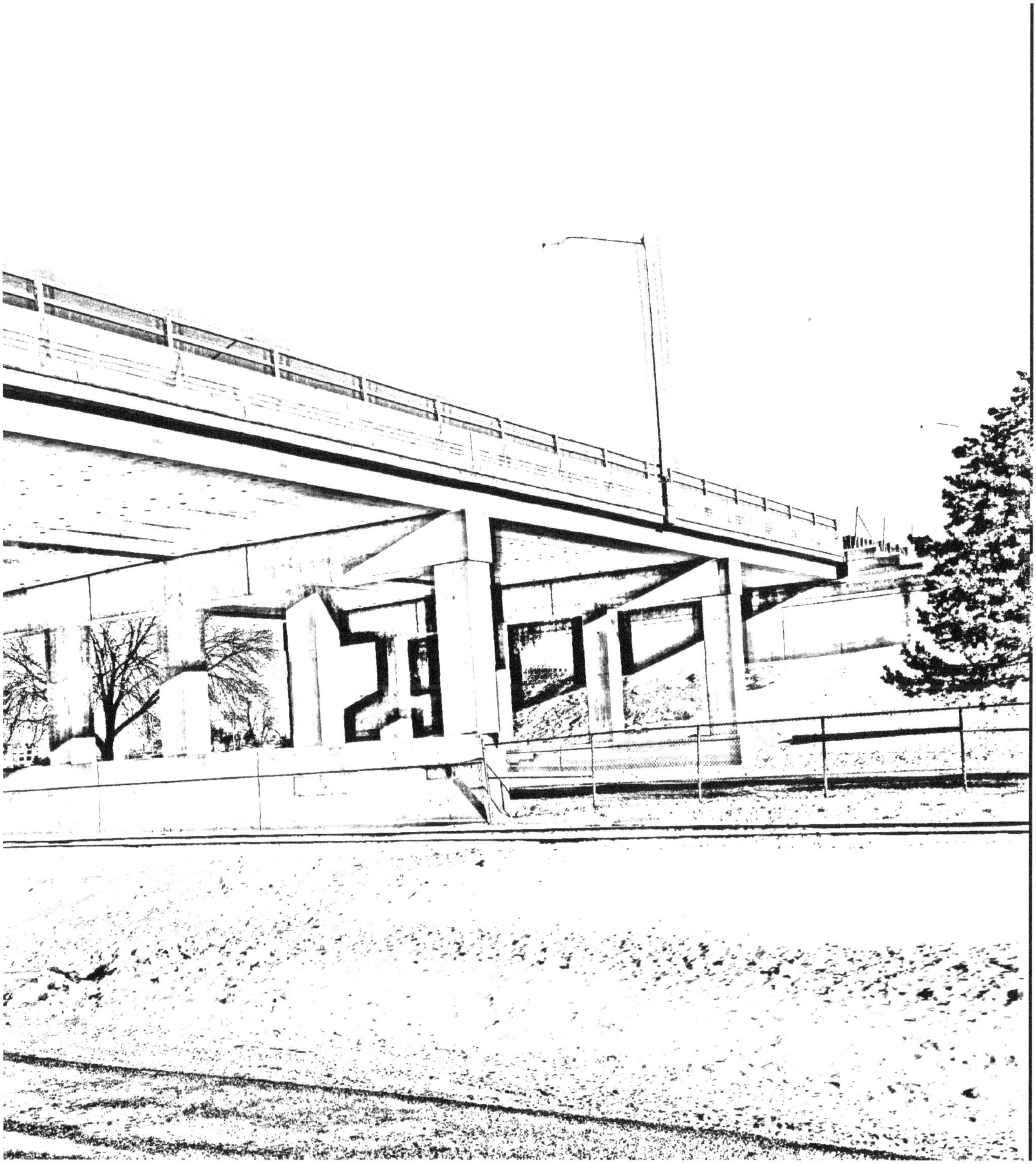

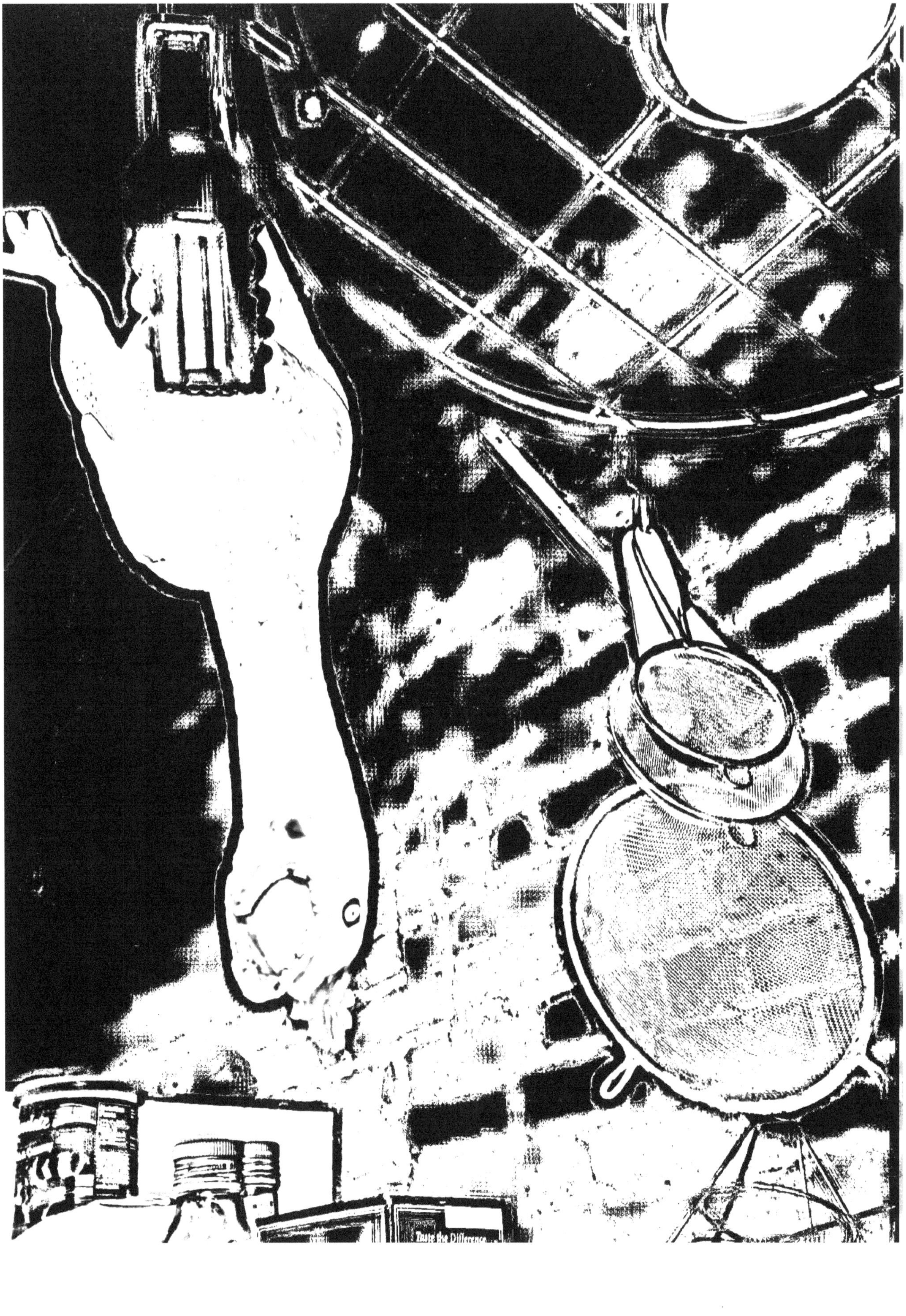
Taste the Difference

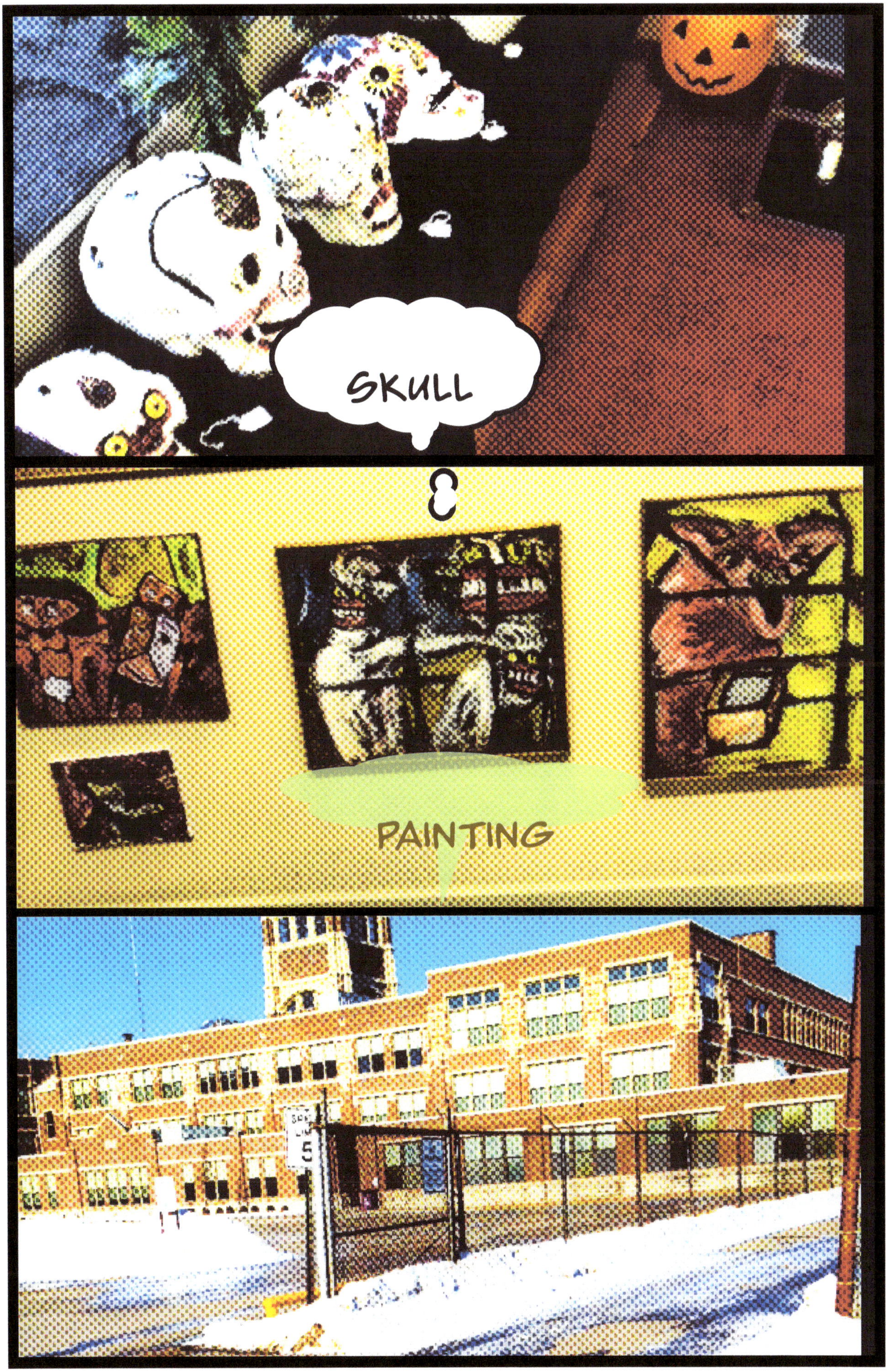
SKULL
PAINTING

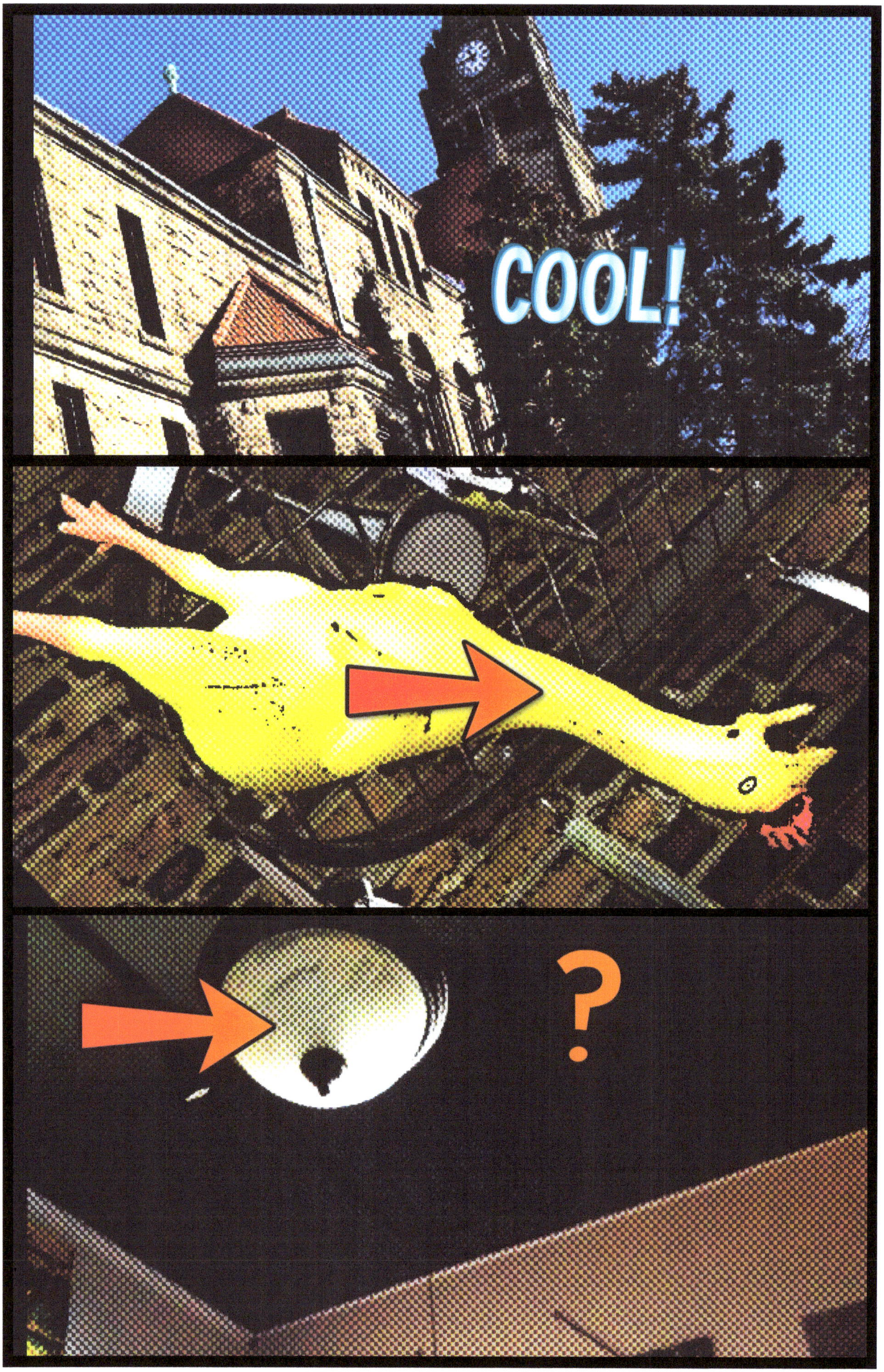
COOL!
?

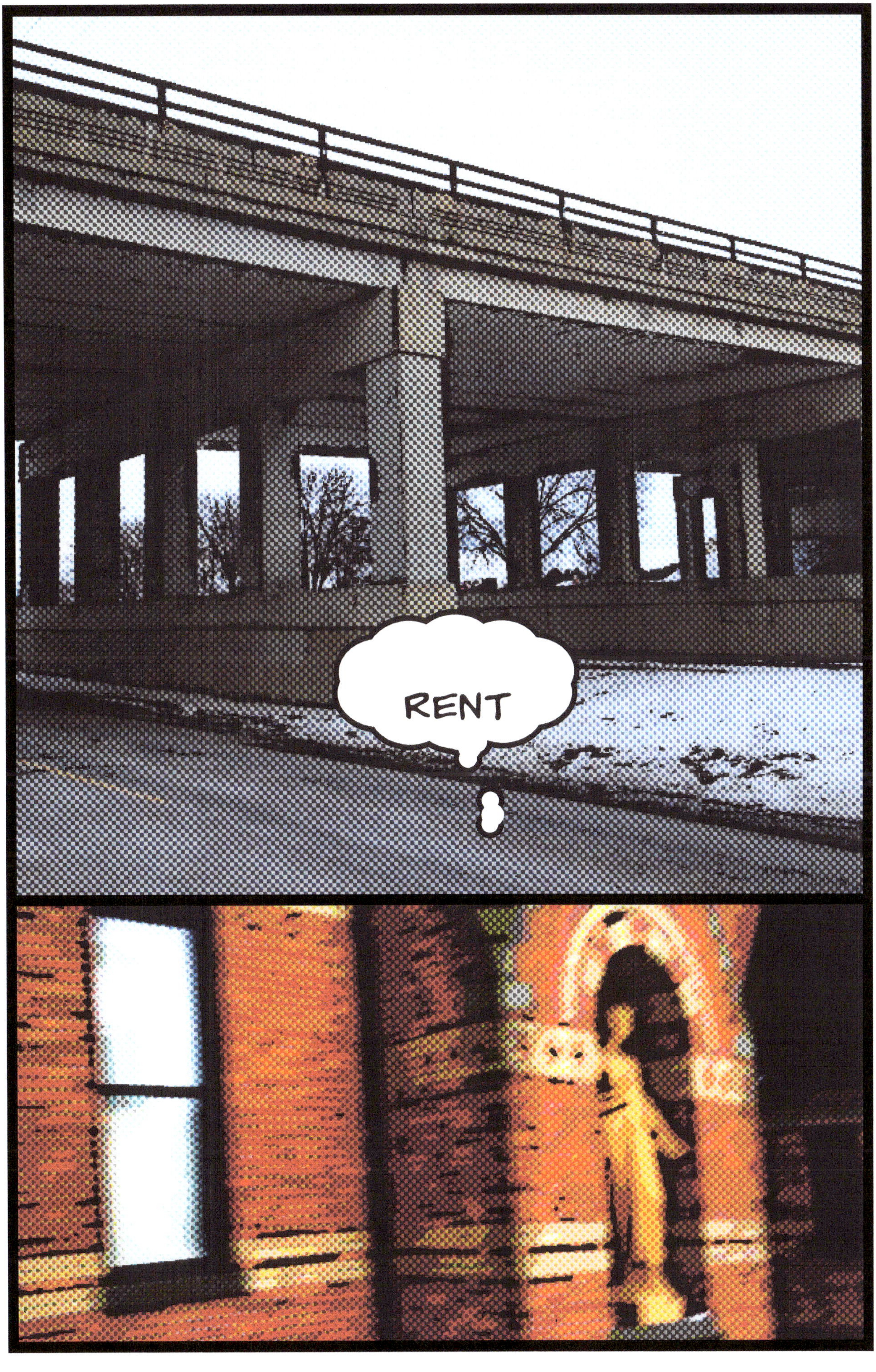
RENT

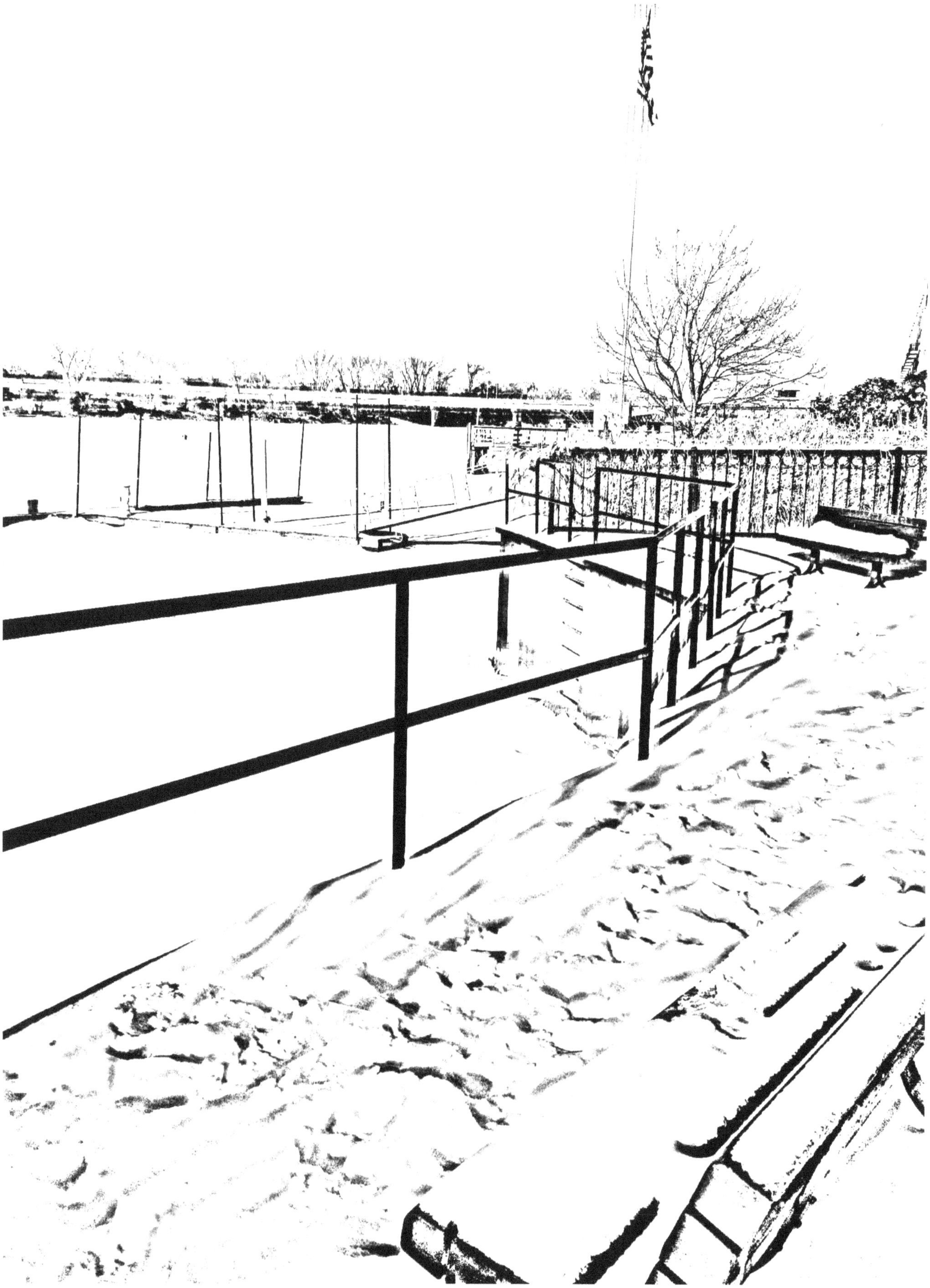

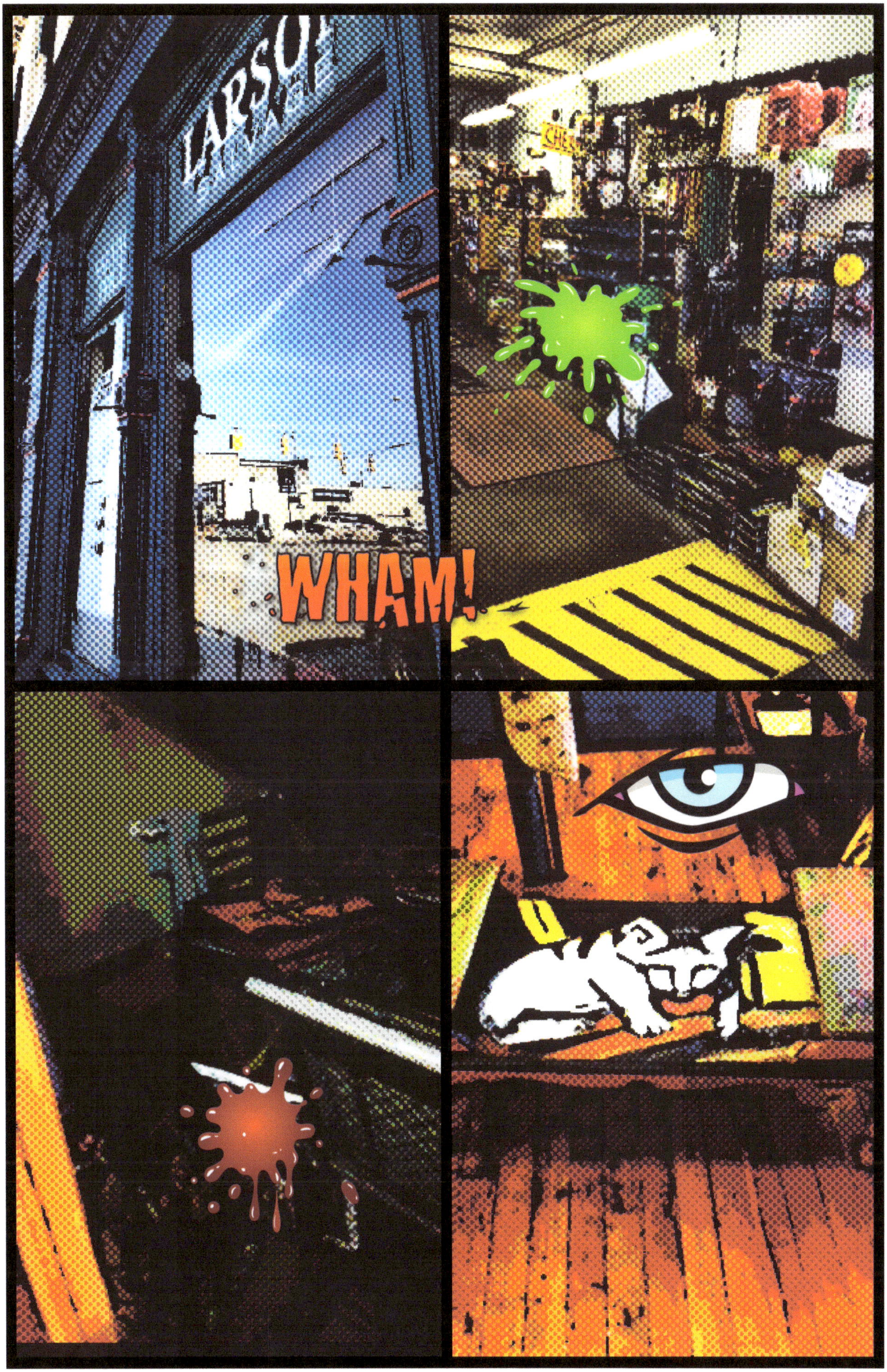
WHAM!

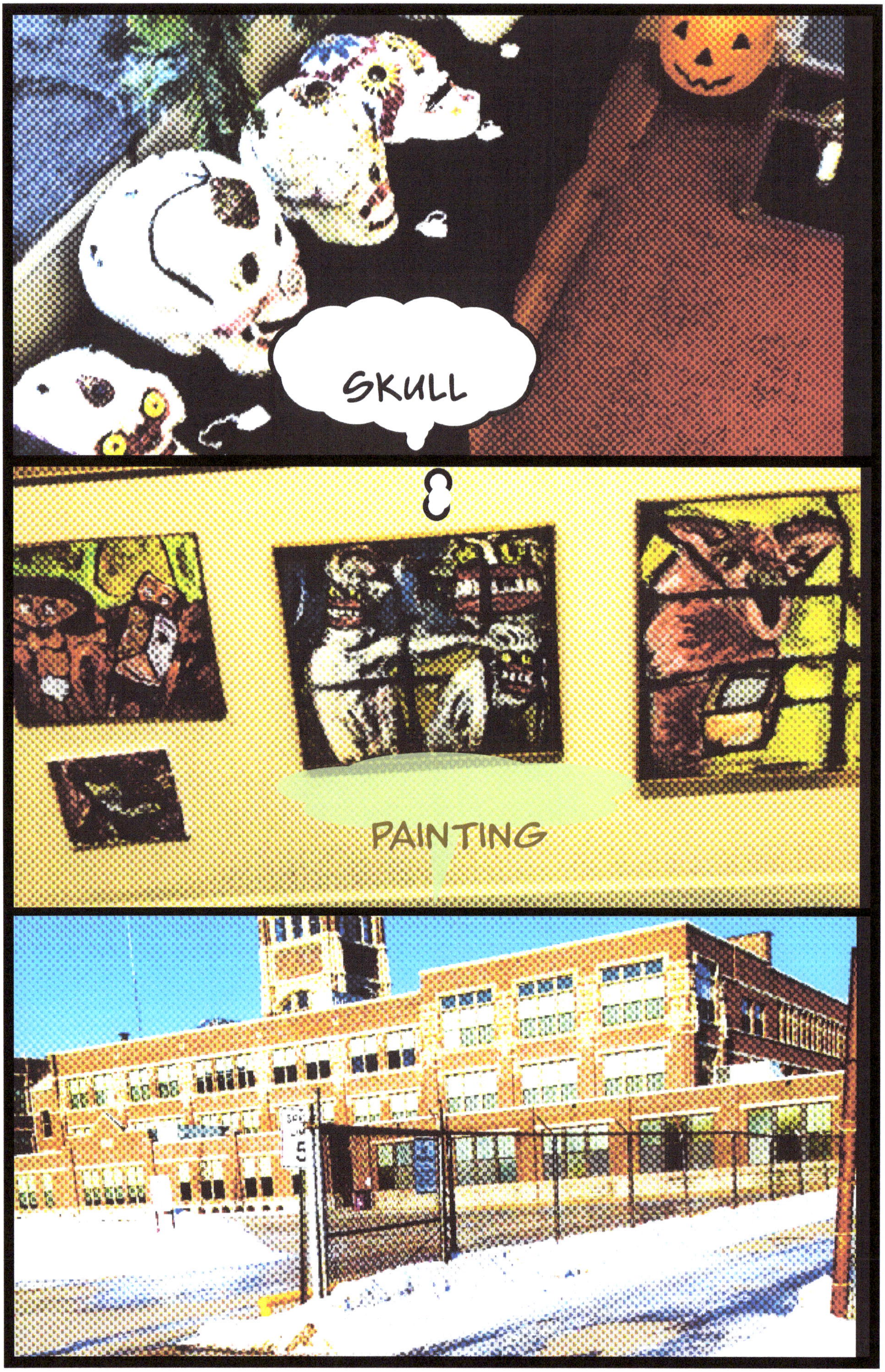
SKULL
PAINTING

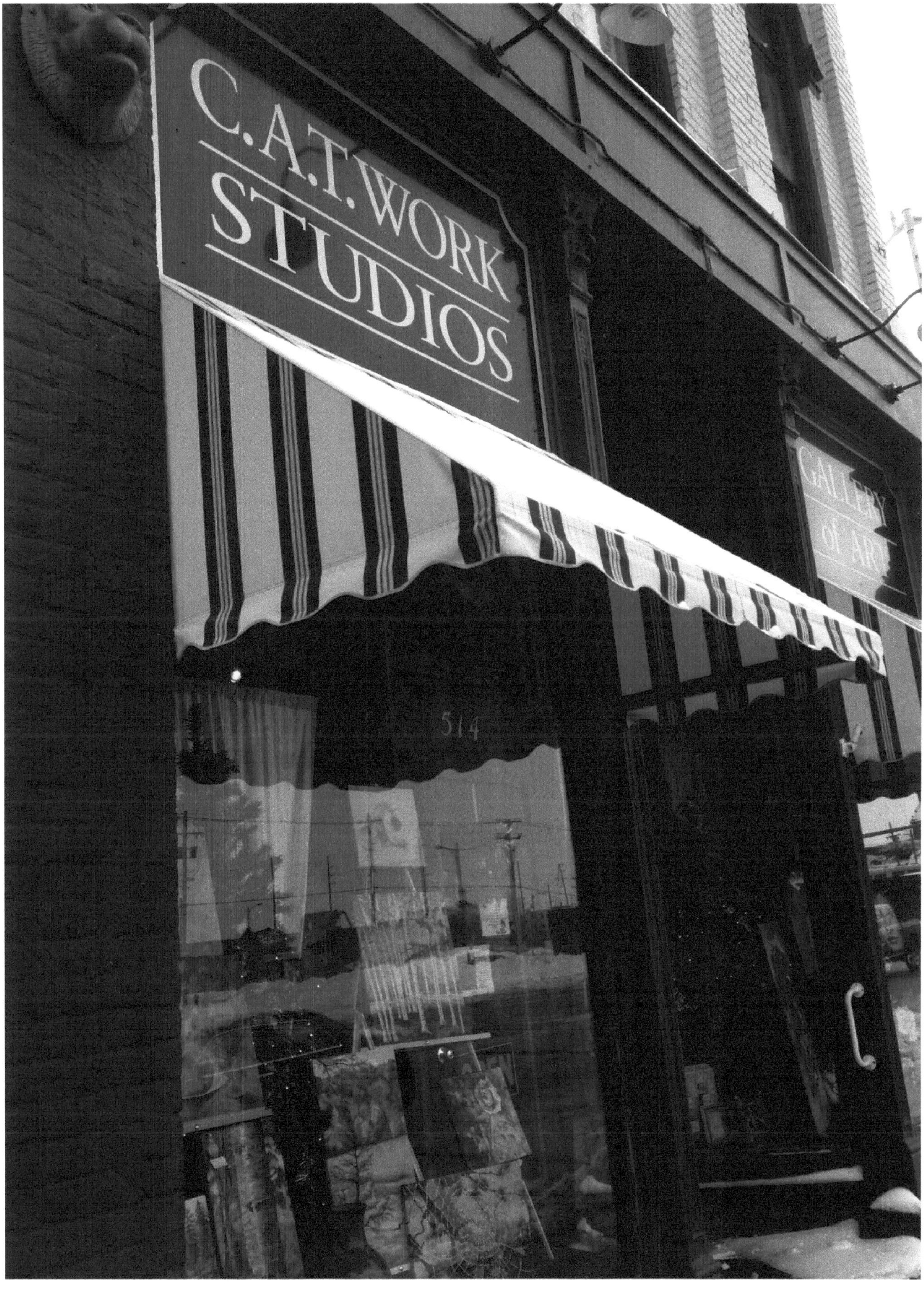
C.A.T. WORK
STUDIOS
514

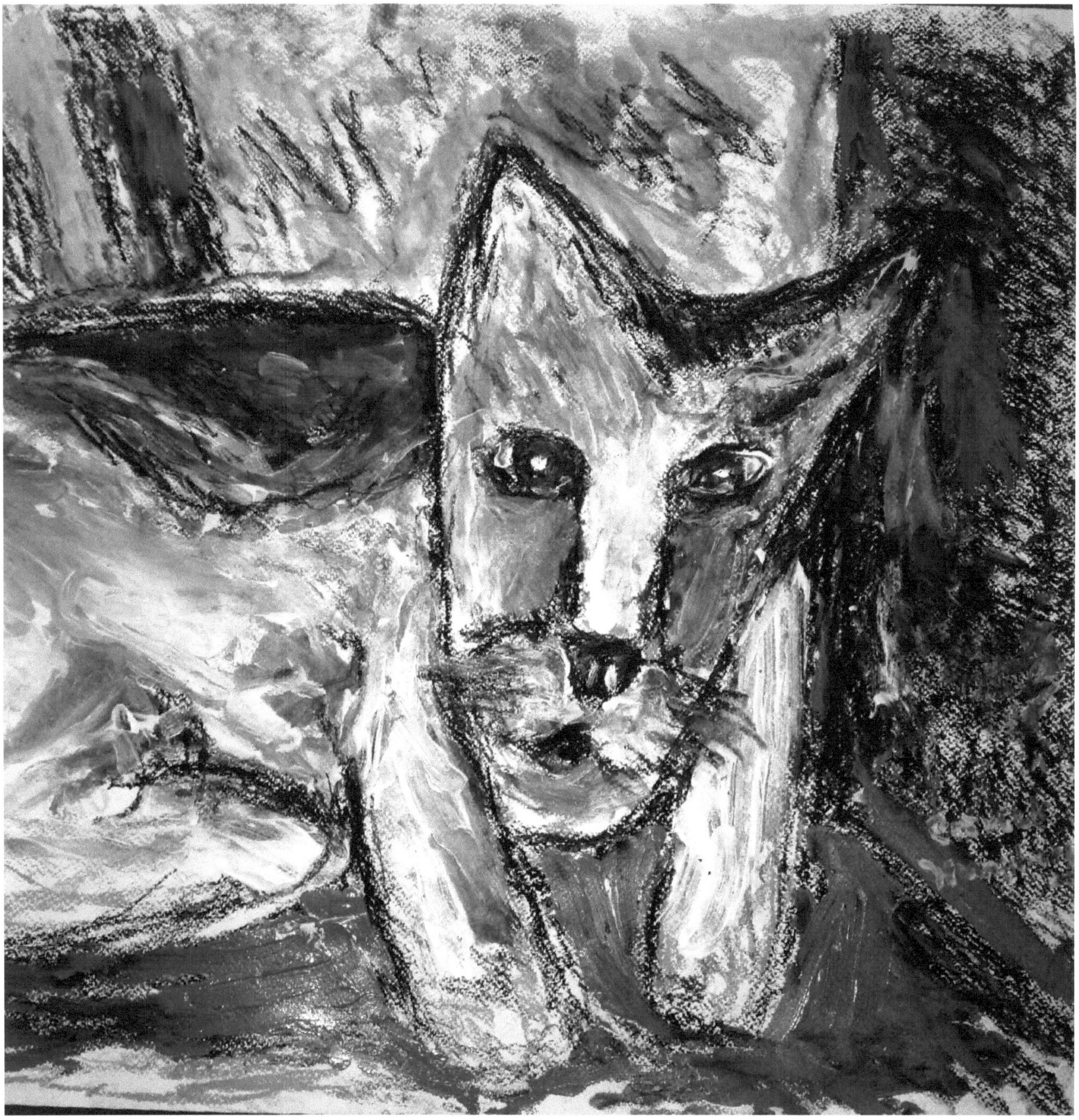

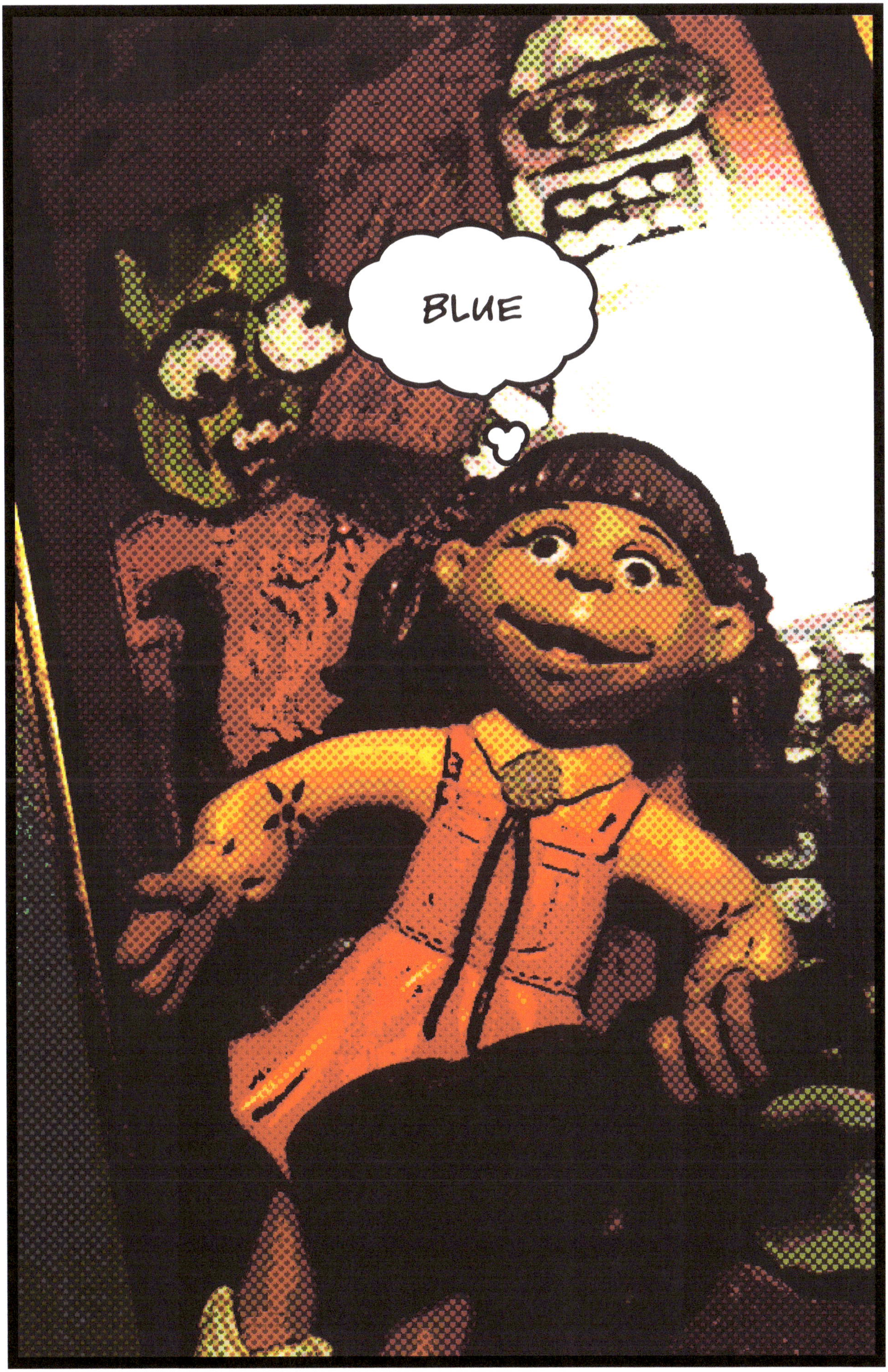
BLUE

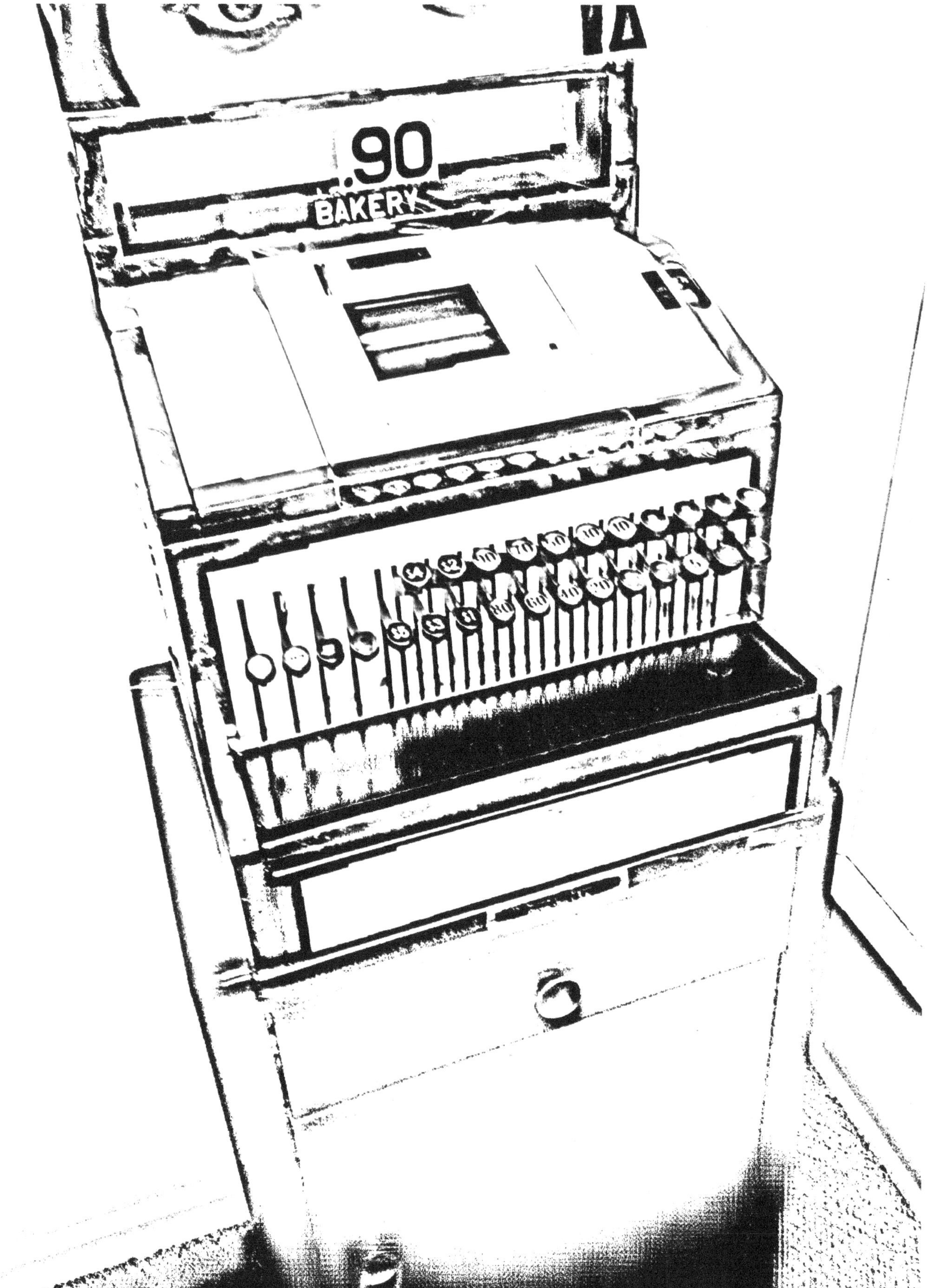
.90
BAKERY

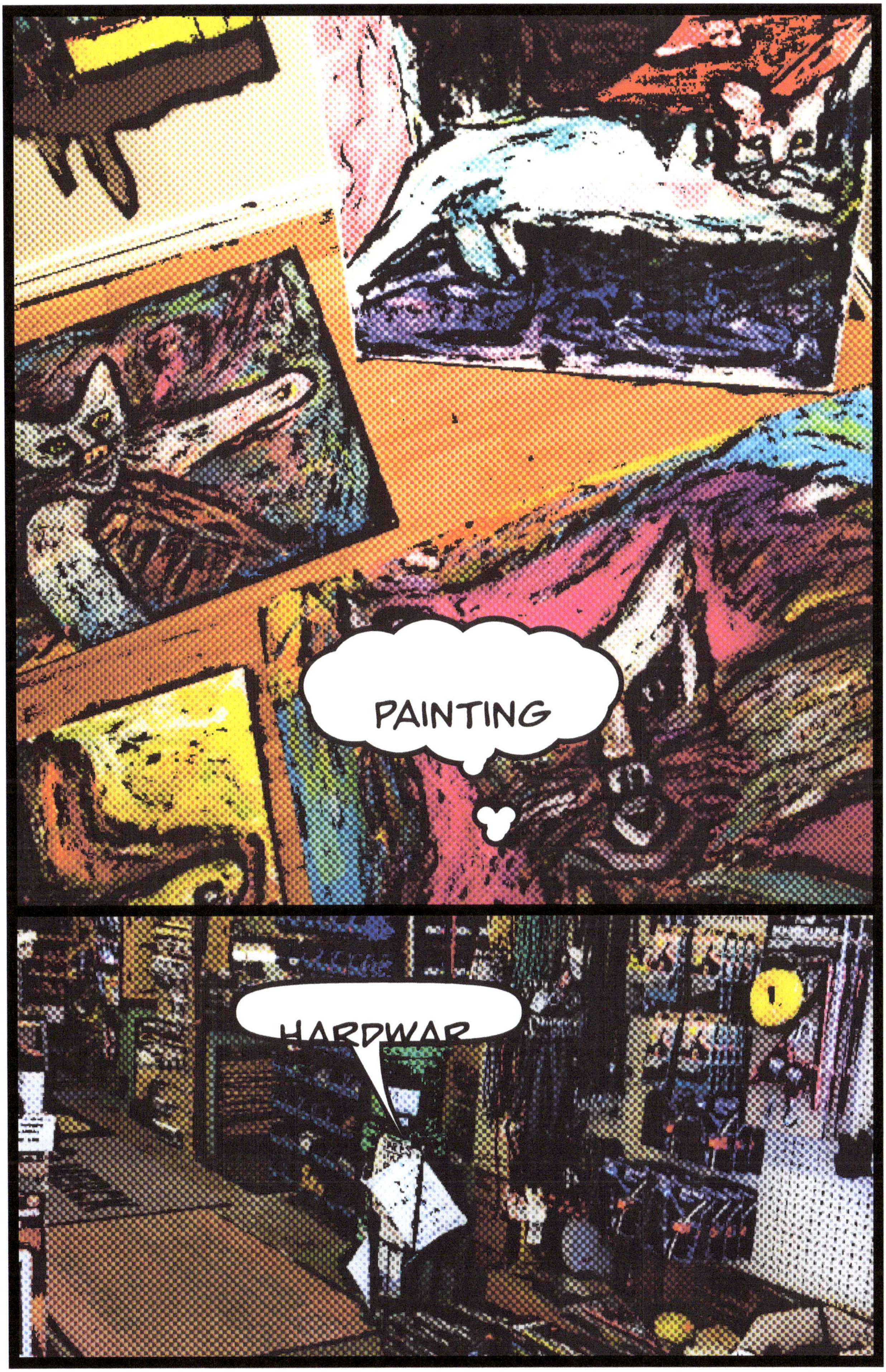
PAINTING
HARDWAR

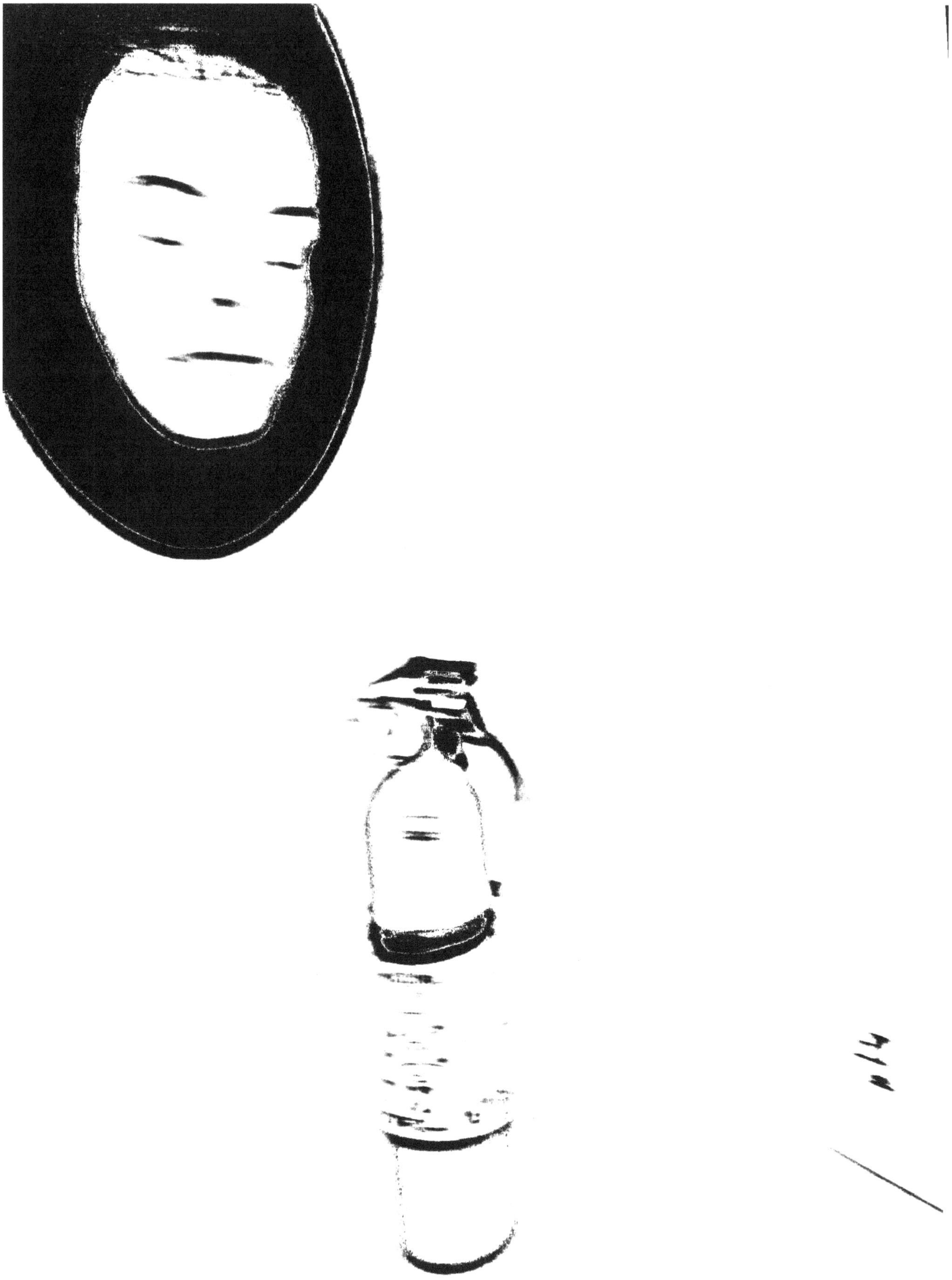

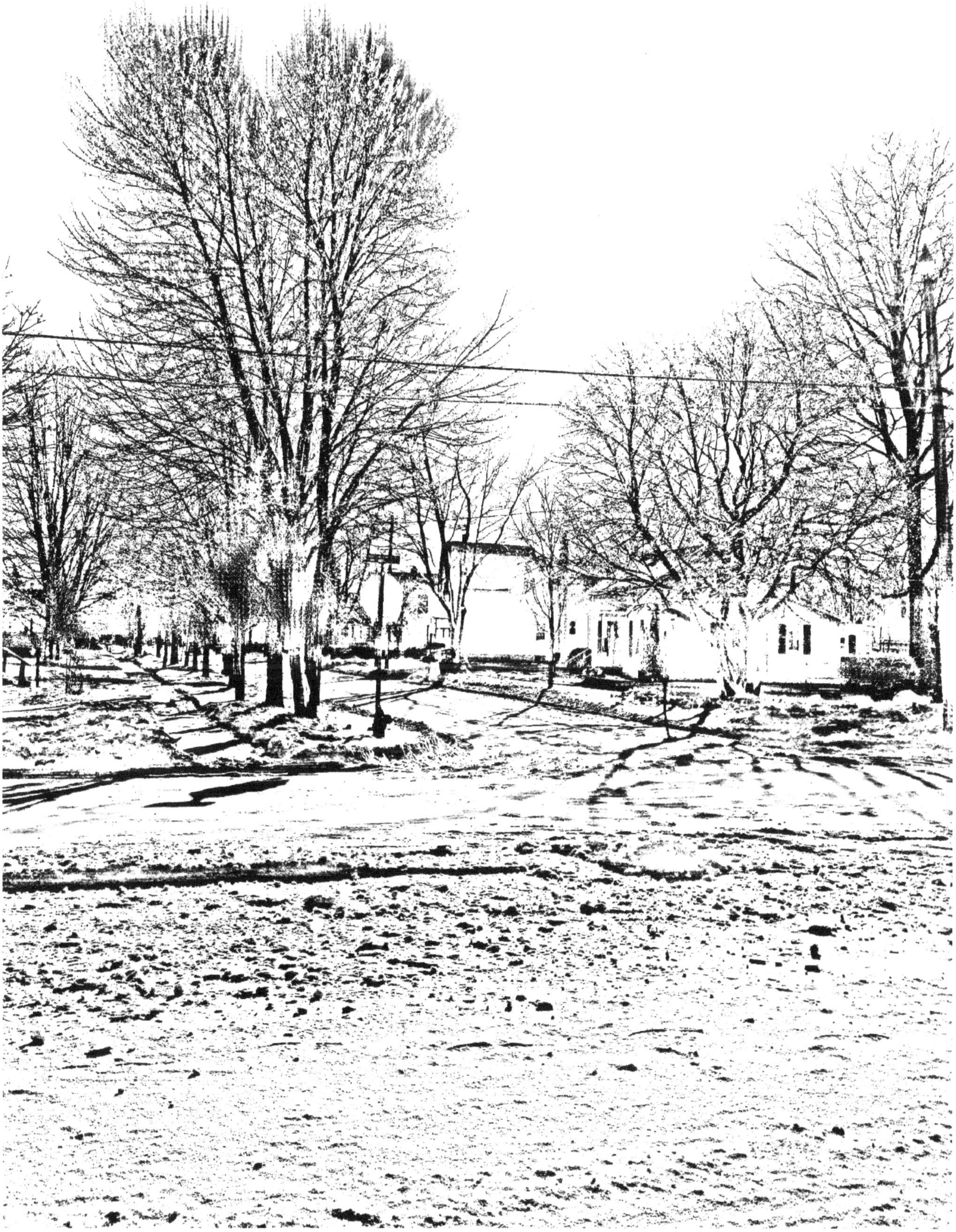

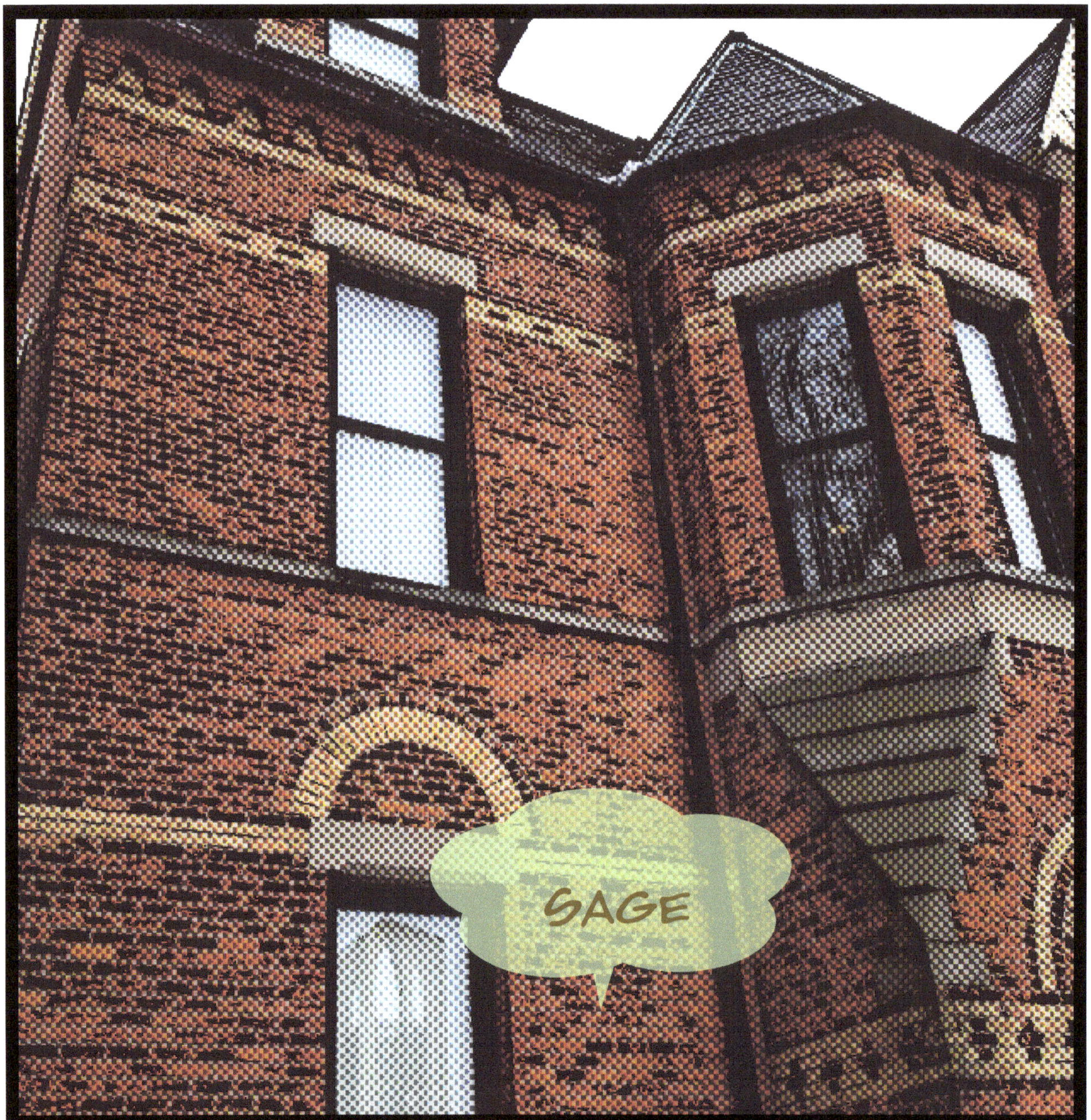
SAGE

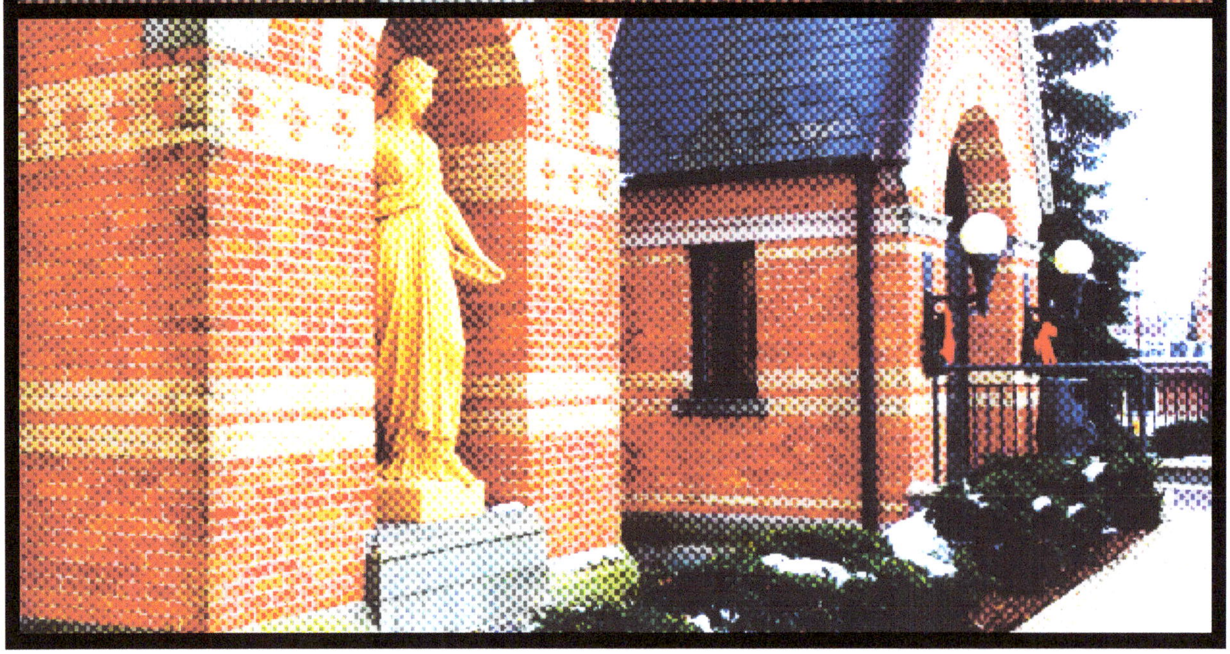

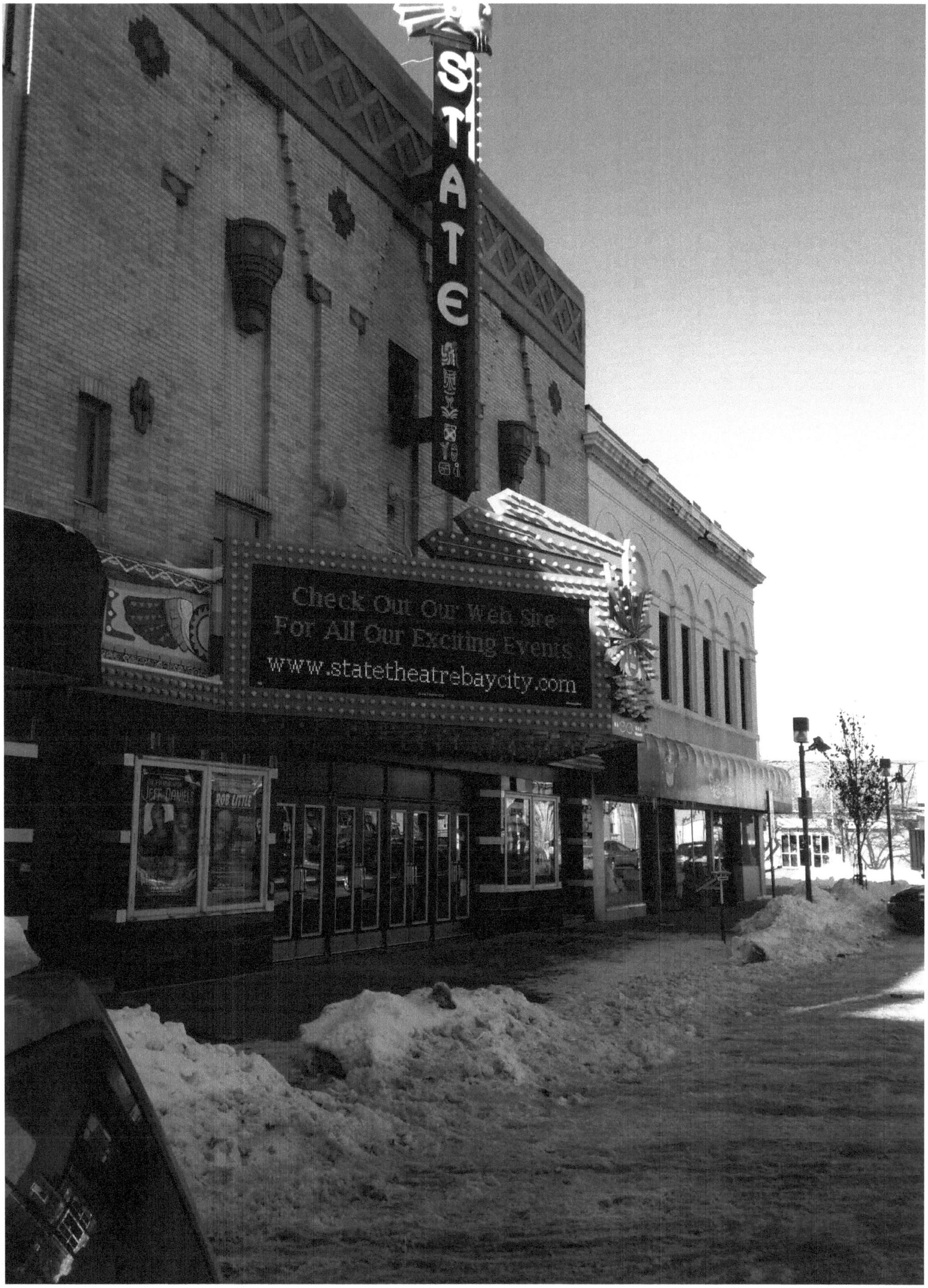
STATE
Check Out Our Web Site
For All Our Exciting Events
www.statetheatrebaycity.com
JEFF DANIELS
ROB LITTLE

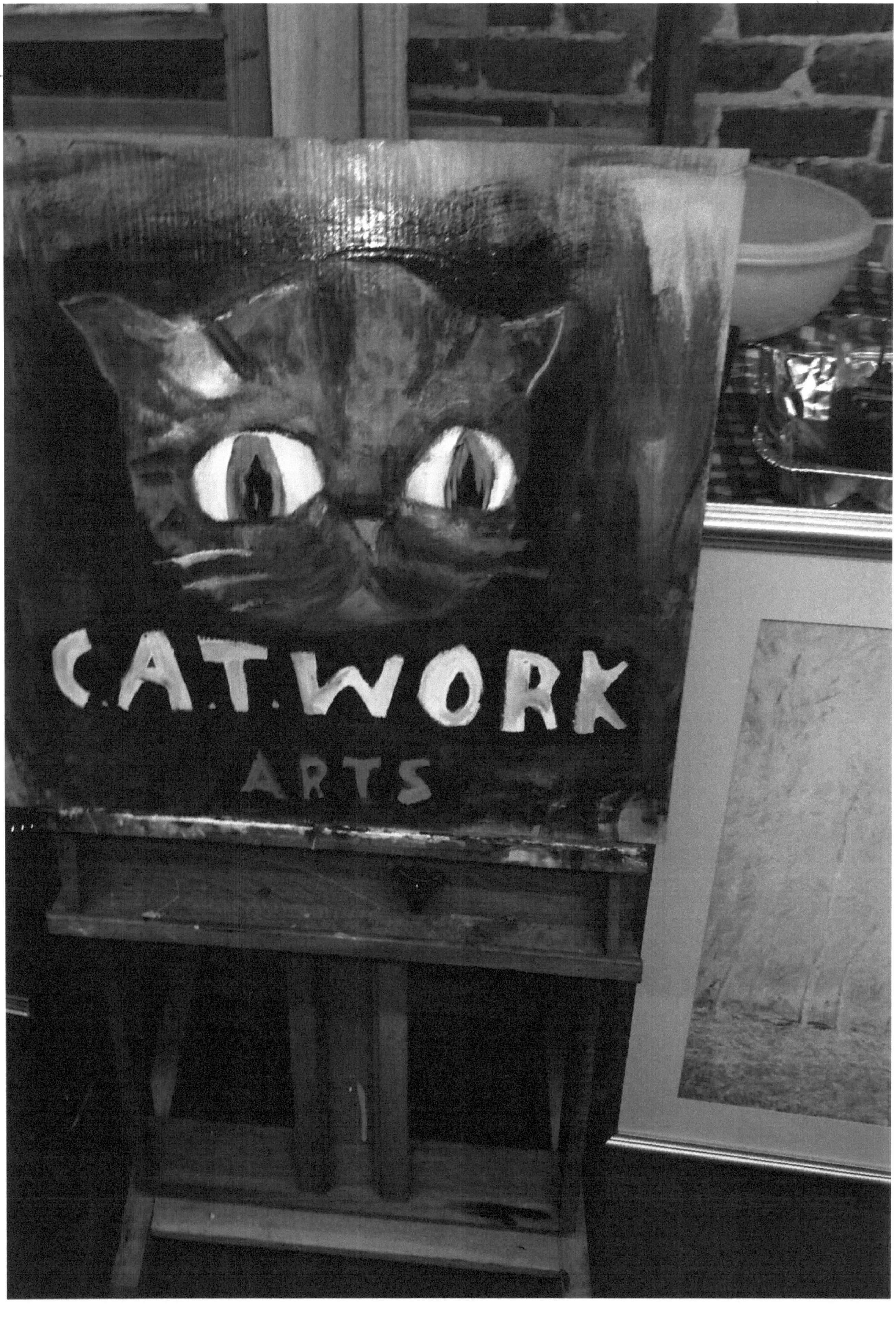
C.A.T. WORK
ARTS

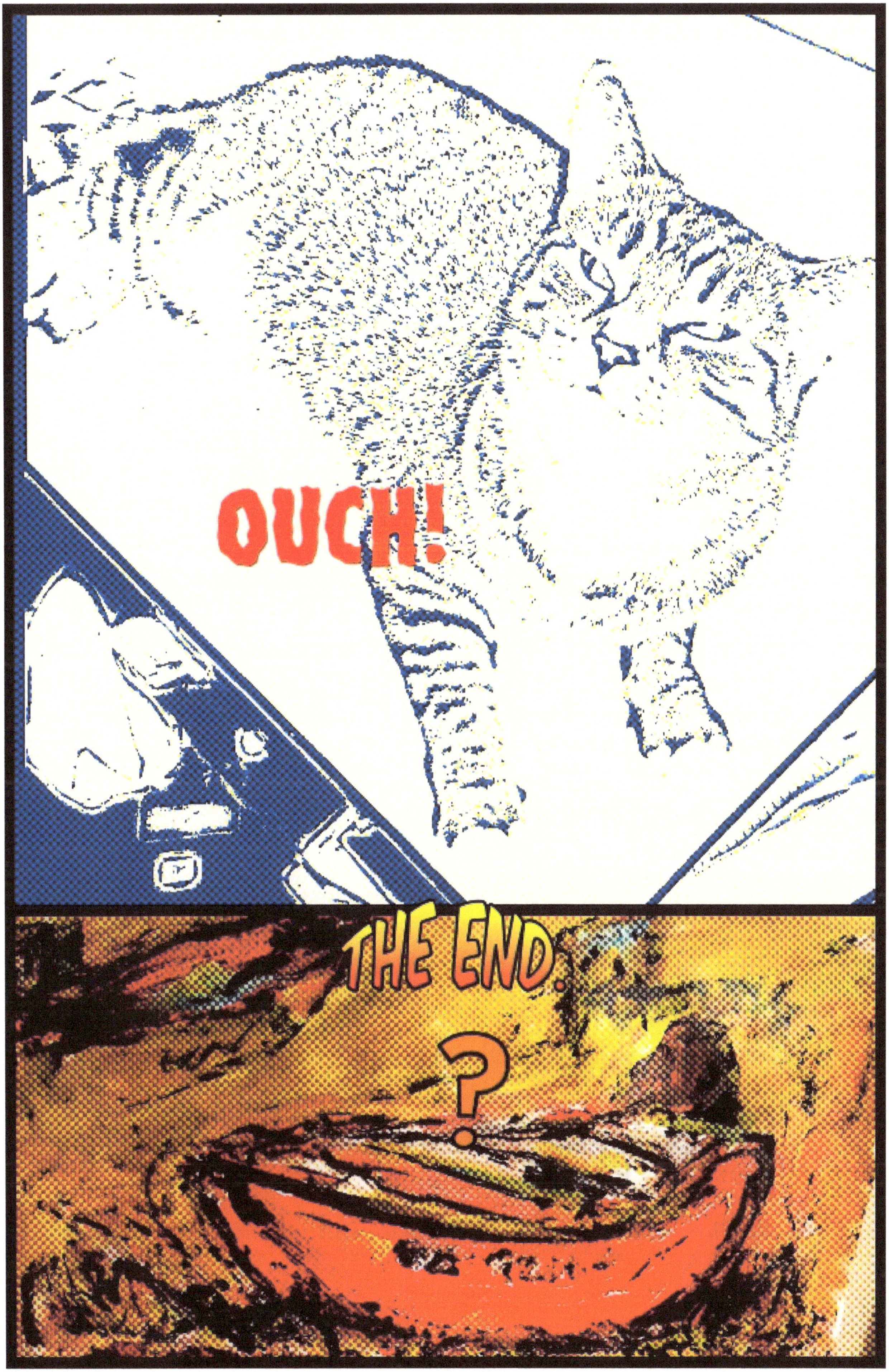
OUCH!
THE END.
?